Mercatus Studies in Politi

Series Editors
Virgil Henry Storr
Mercatus Center
George Mason University
Fairfax, VA, USA

Stefanie Haeffele
Mercatus Center
George Mason University
Fairfax, VA, USA

Political economy is a robust field of study that examines the economic and political institutions that shape our interactions with one another. Likewise, social economy focuses on the social interactions, networks, and communities that embody our daily lives. Together, these fields of study seek to understand the historical and contemporary world around us by examining market, political, and social institutions. Through these sectors of life, people come together to exchange goods and services, solve collective problems, and build communities to live better together.

Scholarship in this tradition is alive and thriving today. By using the lens of political and social economy, books in this series will examine complex social problems, the institutions that attempt to solve these problems, and the consequences of action within such institutions. Further, this approach lends itself to a variety of methods, including fieldwork, case studies, and experimental economics. Such analysis allows for deeper understanding of social phenomena, detailing the context, incentives, and interactions that shape our lives. This series provides a much-needed space for interdisciplinary research on contemporary topics on political and social economy. In much of academia today, scholars are encouraged to work independently and within the strict boundaries of their disciplines. However, the pursuit of understanding our society requires social scientists to collaborate across disciplines, using multiple methods. This series provides such an opportunity for scholars interested in breaking down the boundaries of disciplines in order to better understand the world around us.

More information about this series at
http://www.palgrave.com/gp/series/15998

Stefanie Haeffele • Virgil Henry Storr
Editors

Bottom-up Responses to Crisis

palgrave
macmillan

Editors
Stefanie Haeffele
F. A. Hayek Program for Advanced Study in
Philosophy, Politics, and Economics
Mercatus Center at George Mason University
Fairfax, VA, USA

Virgil Henry Storr
F. A. Hayek Program for Advanced Study in
Philosophy, Politics, and Economics
Mercatus Center at George Mason University
Fairfax, VA, USA

Mercatus Studies in Political and Social Economy
ISBN 978-3-030-39311-3   ISBN 978-3-030-39312-0   (eBook)
https://doi.org/10.1007/978-3-030-39312-0

Cover illustration: © Zoonar GmbH / Alamy Stock Photo

This Palgrave Macmillan imprint is published by the registered company Springer Nature Switzerland AG.
The registered company address is: Gewerbestrasse 11, 6330 Cham, Switzerland

Contents

List of Contributors

Paul Dragos Aligica F. A. Hayek Program for Advanced Study in Philosophy, Politics, and Economics, Mercatus Center at George Mason University, Fairfax, VA, USA

Joshua Ammons Department of Economics, George Mason University, Fairfax, VA, USA

Jessica Austin Department of Sociology, University of Colorado Boulder, Boulder, CO, USA
Natural Hazards Center, University of Colorado Boulder, Boulder, CO, USA

Elizabeth Bittel Department of Sociology, SUNY Cortland, Cortland, NY, USA
South Asia Program, Cornell University, Ithaca, NY, USA

Christopher J. Coyne Department of Economics, George Mason University, Fairfax, VA, USA
F. A. Hayek Program for Advanced Study in Philosophy, Politics, and Economics, Mercatus Center at George Mason University, Fairfax, VA, USA

Simone Domingue Department of Sociology, University of Colorado Boulder, Boulder, CO, USA
Natural Hazards Center, University of Colorado Boulder, Boulder, CO, USA

Laura E. Grube Department of Economics, Beloit College, Beloit, WI, USA

Stefanie Haeffele F. A. Hayek Program for Advanced Study in Philosophy, Politics, and Economics, Mercatus Center at George Mason University, Fairfax, VA, USA

Steven Horwitz Department of Economics, Ball State University, Muncie, IN, USA

Amy LePore Anthem Planning, Inc., Middletown, DE, USA

Ilia Murtazashvili Graduate School of Public and International Affairs, University of Pittsburgh, Pittsburgh, PA, USA

Jennifer Murtazashvili Graduate School of Public and International Affairs, University of Pittsburgh, Pittsburgh, PA, USA

Lori Peek Department of Sociology, University of Colorado Boulder, Boulder, CO, USA
Natural Hazards Center, University of Colorado Boulder, Boulder, CO, USA

Thomas Savidge George Mason University, Fairfax, VA, USA

Virgil Henry Storr Department of Economics, George Mason University, Fairfax, VA, USA
F. A. Hayek Program for Advanced Study in Philosophy, Politics, and Economics, Mercatus Center at George Mason University, Fairfax, VA, USA

Melissa Villarreal Department of Sociology, University of Colorado Boulder, Boulder, CO, USA
Natural Hazards Center, University of Colorado Boulder, Boulder, CO, USA

List of Figures

List of Tables

1

Introduction

Stefanie Haeffele and Virgil Henry Storr

1.1 Introduction

Crises can disrupt and even destroy lives. Think of disasters like hurricanes, earthquakes, fires, and floods. Think of economic crises like episodes of hyperinflation or severe economic downturns. Think of political crises like riots and revolutions. These crises seem to be occurring with increasing frequency in small and large, rich and poor, isolated and connected communities around the globe. Indeed, every individual and community is vulnerable to crises. Whether or not an individual or

S. Haeffele (✉)
F. A. Hayek Program for Advanced Study in Philosophy, Politics, and Economics, Mercatus Center at George Mason University, Fairfax, VA, USA
e-mail: shaeffele@mercatus.gmu.edu

V. H. Storr
Department of Economics, George Mason University, Fairfax, VA, USA

F. A. Hayek Program for Advanced Study in Philosophy, Politics, and Economics, Mercatus Center at George Mason University, Fairfax, VA, USA

© The Author(s) 2020   **1**
S. Haeffele, V. H. Storr (eds.), *Bottom-up Responses to Crisis*, Mercatus Studies in Political and Social Economy, https://doi.org/10.1007/978-3-030-39312-0_1

community succeeds or fails, thrives or flounders, prospers or struggles will depend in part on how they respond to these crises.

Effectively responding to crises, however, can be a daunting challenge. Consider, for instance, Hurricane Katrina which devastated New Orleans, Louisiana, and much of the Gulf Coast, in August of 2005. Hurricane Katrina and the flooding that followed resulted in over 1800 deaths and $100 billion in damages (Knabb et al. 2006). New Orleans suffered the worst damage. As much as 80 percent of the city was flooded, 70 percent of the housing units were damaged, and around 600,000 residents were still displaced a month after the storm.[1] Recovering from a disaster of this scale and scope is extremely difficult for displaced disaster survivors. While the benefits of returning and rebuilding are necessarily uncertain, the costs of returning and rebuilding a damaged or destroyed home can be extremely costly. Returning and rebuilding only makes sense if key goods and services that they need to live are going to be available and other key people and institutions that they rely on also return and rebuild. Individuals within the community must assess the damage to their homes, determine if they are likely to have a place to work and socialize, and if they wish to return, must find ways to work with others from their community to rebuild. Business owners and government officials must figure out if they will have a community to serve and will need to make decisions about where and when to reopen their business or restart public services. In this scenario, the rational move for disaster survivors is to wait and see what others do before committing to a particular recovery strategy. Because of this situation where rebuilding in the wake of a disaster is only rational if others rebuild as well, Storr et al. (2015) and others have described post-disaster recovery as a collective action problem.

Similar challenges are faced by citizens and governments alike during post-war reconstruction, economic recessions, and other types of crises. Yet, we see individuals and communities rebounding from crises all the time. As John Stuart Mill ([1848] 1885, 94–95) remarked, the "great rapidity with which countries recover from a state of devastation" is something of a marvel but is also quite common. Likewise, we see individuals rebounding from crises again and again. How do individuals and communities go about returning to normalcy and beginning again the mundane life of everyday affairs after a crisis? Arguably, effectively responding to crises often requires that the individuals affected find ways to work with one another. Effectively responding to crises also often requires mobilizing significant resources.

Not surprisingly, individuals and communities often turn to government in response to crises. In the wake of crises, governments seem like the only entities who have the resources to meaningfully help survivors and the capability to restore disrupted services or provide needed goods and services. National and supranational governmental organizations are often seen as being in the best position to identify the problems, understand the circumstances, provide resources, direct action, and coordinate among the various constituencies following a major crisis. Governments, however, can themselves be overwhelmed by crises, depending on their scale and scope. Moreover, government can sometimes be the cause of the crisis and some might not be well positioned to provide the solution to the crisis. In these circumstances, individuals and communities must depend on bottom-up solutions.

This volume examines an important aspect of responding to crises that is often overlooked by media and policymakers—the potential and capabilities of bottom-up efforts. This volume provides an overview of the literature on bottom-up crisis responses, highlights the lessons learned from several studies of particular bottom-up crisis responses, and provides a framework for future research and policy discussions on the potential of individuals and their communities to participate in and drive their own crisis response efforts.

1.2 Why Bottom-Up Response and Recovery Efforts Matter

Due to the scale and scope of crises—often resulting in large-scale destruction and uncertainty at the community, state, and national level—it is not surprising that there are consistent calls from citizens, the media, scholars, and policymakers for government involvement. Centralized government authority (either the federal government, other national governments, or supranational governmental organizations) is often viewed as necessary for leading and coordinating crisis response efforts in order to bring together and prioritize efforts from many constituencies and for providing the resources (such as funding, qualified personnel, infrastructure, and equipment) needed to respond effectively (see Pipa 2006; Tierney 2007; Thaler and Sunstein 2008; Springer 2009; Fakhruddin and Chivakidakarn 2014; Coppola 2015). Further, crises (such as natural disasters) can lead to communication system failures, can expose security vulnerabilities, and are often caused by and can exacerbate systemic environmental issues that seem beyond the ability of any individual to address. These complications only bolster the calls for government involvement.

It is increasingly difficult, however, to centrally or cohesively train for, mitigate against, and respond to the complicated circumstances caused by crises. To fully understand, coordinate, and respond to crises, central authorities (just like individuals and communities) must be able to (1) access information about the damage on the ground and resources available, (2) prioritize and initiate activities, and (3) adapt when circumstances change. There is a robust literature pointing to the challenges of a central authority's ability to access and utilize dispersed knowledge and resources (see Mises [1920] 1990; Hayek 1945; Lavoie 1985a) and to adjust when errors or changes occur (see Kirzner 1985; Lavoie 1985b; Ikeda 2005). These challenges, arguably, are exacerbated in times of crises, when communication systems are hindered and information about the extent of the damage and individuals impacted may be uncertain or change dramatically over time. Indeed, after a crisis like a hurricane or earthquake, central authorities tend to face challenges identifying and assessing needs and coordinating resources in the immediate response. Government personnel can take days to weeks to arrive, to assess the situation, and begin to provide goods and services to those in need. Additionally, recovery plans tend to take a long time to compile, face backlash when released, and are revised, which can all delay actual recovery (see Sobel and Leeson 2007; Coyne 2008, 2013; Chamlee-Wright 2010; Haeffele-Balch and Storr 2015; Storr et al. 2015).

While the media, the public, and policymakers often turn to government for the official response after a crisis, the individuals directly impacted by a crisis must find ways to stay safe, contact their loved ones, assess the damage, and figure out what to do next. In other words, the survivors of a disaster must go about response and recovery no matter if an official government response and recovery effort takes place or not. Given this, and the real challenges central authorities face, it is important to examine how individuals go about participating in their own recovery as well as their limitations and potential for success.

Individuals and local organizations who come together to respond to crises can be said to bring about recovery from the bottom-up. Their focused efforts utilize their social capital and networks and their skills and expertise to obtain information on the challenges they face and to coordinate with others (see Bolin and Stanford 1998; Hurlbert et al. 2000, 2001; Shaw and Goda 2004; Paton 2007; Chamlee-Wright 2010; Aldrich 2012; Storr et al. 2015). Their approaches allow for information sharing, error correction, and ultimately, social learning (see Chamlee-Wright 2010; Storr et al. 2015, 2017). Moreover, bottom-up efforts provide the experiences and capacity for becoming more resilient communities (see Chamlee-Wright 2010; Aldrich 2012; Burton 2014; Storr et al. 2015).

Local entrepreneurs and community leaders—such as pastors, business owners, and local government officials—play an important role in connecting disparate residents, inspiring others to commit to recovery, voicing the opinions and expectations of the community, and providing needed goods and services (see Chamlee-Wright 2010; Storr et al. 2015). Perhaps surprisingly, even big businesses—such as Walmart, Tide, and others—are drivers of response and recovery by giving local managers autonomy to best serve their communities, shifting inventory to geographical areas in need, and investing resources back into the community (see Horwitz 2009). Likewise, entrepreneurs, businesses, and charities seeking to help those in need are more likely to connect to individuals who seek aid if they have connections to the affected community.

The disaster literature rightly raises cause for concern about the ability of certain groups to recover compared to others. For instance, minorities, the poor, and marginalized groups are less likely to be prepared for crises, tend to suffer more injuries and deaths from crises, and have a harder time accessing resources and recovering from crises (see Wright 1979; Hewitt 1997; Blanchard-Boehm 1998; Norris et al. 1999; Peacock 2003; Fothergill 2004; Wisner et al. 2004). There are strands of the literature, however, that have added nuance to the traditional perception of vulnerable populations and how they can contribute to and get assistance with recovery. For instance, children are more capable of participating in response and recovery efforts than might first be believed (see Fothergill and Peek 2015; Peek 2008). Likewise, while developing nations suffer more deaths than more developed, wealthier nations (see Kahn 2005), their citizens still find ways to adapt to changing circumstances and do their best to respond and recover from crises. Research has shown that individuals and communities in weak and failed states develop self-governing institutions (see Leeson 2014; Murtazashvili 2016), participate in entrepreneurship in hostile environments in order to provide and obtain goods and services (see Galbraith and Stiles 2006; Bullough et al. 2013), and find unique ways to overcome crises. While these populations can benefit from better institutions, economic progress, and support from their fellow residents and government, they are more capable than sometimes perceived and do, indeed, participate in their own recovery. Bottom-up efforts are, thus, worthy of study as well as worthy of being recognized and given the space to act in the post-crisis context.

1.3   Summary of Chapters in the Volume

The chapters in this volume highlight the ingenuity and persistence of individuals and private organizations to participate in their own crisis response and recovery in developed nations, such as the United States, as well as weak and failed states. Together, the chapters argue that there are many ways that local leaders, entrepreneurs, and citizens pursue bottom-up responses to crises, by examining the capabilities, feedback mechanisms, and network effects of decentralized efforts. The contributors in this volume are accomplished scholars and seasoned practitioners who have spent time in the field learning how theory meets practice in crises management as well as spanning multiple disciplines including sociology, economics, and public administration.

Providing overarching frameworks for studying bottom-up responses to crises, Chap. 2 outlines the literature on how bottom-up efforts function in the post-disaster context and Chap. 3 poses nonviolent action as a specific form of bottom-up response to crises. In Chap. 2, Laura E. Grube outlines the "what, how, and why" of bottom-up responses to disasters and argues that such efforts are just as important as the centralized efforts that permeate the popular view of disaster response. Specifically, by reviewing the contemporary literature on bottom-up recovery and using case studies from Hurricanes Katrina and Sandy, Grube shows how such efforts provide goods, services, and information as well as coordinate and encourage recovery because they can access local knowledge, utilize social capital, and adapt when circumstances change. People turn to and mobilize their own bottom-up recovery efforts because they know and trust their neighbors and community and are able to utilize the organizations, resources, and skills that they have on hand, just as they often do during mundane times. Fully recognizing the role of bottom-up efforts in disaster recovery implies that policymakers should find ways ensure and encourage that people can have the space to participate in and drive their own recovery.

Joshua Ammons and Christopher J. Coyne argue that nonviolent action is an important form of bottom-up response to crises in Chap. 3. They review the literature on nonviolent action. The methods of nonviolent action can provide a check against state power and threats of war or invasion, and provide alternative options to those who are oppressed or abandoned in times of crises. This framework can improve our understanding of the capacity of bottom-up response and the incentives and circumstances necessary for successful change, and allow for deeper analysis of the methods bottom-up actors engage in when fighting against centralized plans or trying to get collective attention after crises.

The next three chapters explore the role of businesses, local emergency managers, and children in crisis response and recovery. In Chap. 4, Steven Horwitz discusses how businesses, particularly big businesses like Walmart and McDonald's, respond after disasters by quickly reopening their stores, giving way goods and services to those in need, and ensuring autonomy to local managers to do what is best for their community. Amy LePore, in Chap. 5, discusses the potential and challenges of local emergency management to implement public-private partnerships. Despite the recognition and encouragement of such partnerships from the federal level through FEMA's 2010 Whole Community doctrine, local emergency management is constrained by their reliance on federal funding and command-and-control models that weaken their ability to build partnerships and distribute authority. And in Chap. 6, Lori Peek, Jessica Austin, Elizabeth Bittel, Simone Domingue, and Melissa Villarreal document that children and youth, who are often only considered to be young and vulnerable victims of disaster, actively participate in disaster efforts, including risk reduction, preparedness, and recovery. Children do not just passively experience and are impacted by disasters but are capable of voicing their concerns, participating in recovery, and advocating for broader social change.

The volume then turns to state-level crises, with an examination of bottom-up state-building and the potential for bottom-up responses to state-induced crises. In Chap. 7, Jennifer Murtazashvili and Ilia Murtazashvili counter the prevailing emphasis of the importance of national-level state-building for fixing fragile states with what they call "bottom-up state building," which focuses on local political institutions, economic reform, and partnership with customary and tribal institutions. They use Afghanistan as an example, highlighting the issues that arise when international organizations ignore and dissuade the power of bottom-up institutional reform. Finally, Paul Dragos Aligica and Thomas Savidge, in Chap. 8, examine how states can induce political and economic crises that can result in political instability, economic downturns, famine, and death (known as a shortage economy). When faced with such sustained hardship, people find ways to respond to crises to obtain food, medicine, and other essential goods. Yet, broader institutional reforms are needed in order to not just survive within but overcome a shortage economy.

Note

1. This data is from The Data Center (formerly the Greater New Orleans Community Data Center), available online at http://www.datacenterresearch.org/data-resources/katrina/facts-for-impact/.

References

Aldrich, D. 2012. *Building Resilience Social Capital in Post-Disaster Recovery.* Chicago: University of Chicago Press.

Blanchard-Boehm, R.D. 1998. Understanding Public Response to Increased Risk from Natural Hazards: Application of the Hazards Risk Communication Framework. *International Journal of Mass Emergencies and Disasters* 16 (3): 247–278.

Bolin, R., and L. Stanford. 1998. The Northridge Earthquake: Community-Based Approaches to Unmet Recovery Needs. *Disasters* 22 (1): 21–38.

Bullough, A., M. Renko, and T. Myatt. 2013. Danger Zone Entrepreneurs: The Importance of Resilience and Self-Efficiency for Entrepreneurial Intentions. *Entrepreneurship Theory and Practice* 38 (3): 473–499.

Burton, C.G. 2014. A Validation of Metrics for Community Resilience to Natural Hazards and Disasters Using the Recovery from Hurricane Katrina as a Case Study. *Annals of the Association of American Geographers* 105 (1): 67–86.

Chamlee-Wright, E. 2010. *The Cultural and Political Economy of Recovery.* New York: Routledge.

Coppola, D. 2015. *Introduction to International Disaster Management.* Oxford: Elsevier.

Coyne, C.J. 2008. *After War: The Political Economy of Exporting Democracy.* Stanford: Stanford University Press.

———. 2013. *Doing Bad by Doing Good: Why Humanitarian Action Fails.* Stanford: Stanford University Press.

Fakhruddin, S.H.M., and Y. Chivakidakarn. 2014. A Case Study for Early Warning and Disaster Management in Thailand. *International Journal of Disaster Risk Reduction* 9: 159–180.

Fothergill, A. 2004. *Heads Above Water: Gender, Class, and Family in the Grand Forks Flood.* Albany, NY: SUNY Press.

Fothergill, A., and L. Peek. 2015. *Children of Katrina.* Austin: University of Texas Press.

Galbraith, C.S., and C.H. Stiles. 2006. Disasters and Entrepreneurship: A Short Review. *International Research in the Business Disciplines* 5: 147–166.

Haeffele-Balch, S., and V.H. Storr. 2015. Austrian Contributions to the Literature on Natural and Unnatural Disasters. In *New Thinking in Austrian Political Economy (Advances in Austrian Economics)*, ed. C.J. Coyne and V.H. Storr, vol. 19. Bingley, UK: Emerald.

Hayek, F.A. 1945. The Use of Knowledge in Society. *The American Economic Review* 35 (4): 519–530.

Hewitt, K. 1997. *Regions of Risk: A Geographical Introduction to Disasters*. Boston: Addison Wesley Longman.

Horwitz, S. 2009. Wal-Mart to the Rescue: Private Enterprise's Response to Hurricane Katrina. *The Independent Review* 13 (4): 511–528.

Hurlbert, J., V. Haines, and J. Beggs. 2000. Core Networks and Tie Activation: What Kinds of Routine Networks Allocate Resources in Nonroutine Situations? *American Sociological Review* 65 (4): 598–618.

Hurlbert, J., J. Beggs, and V. Haines. 2001. Social Capital in Extreme Environments. In *Social Capital: Theory and Research*, ed. N. Lin, K. Cook, and R. Burt. New York: Aldine De Gruyter.

Ikeda, S. 2005. The Dynamics of Interventionism. *Advances in Austrian Economics* 8: 21–57.

Kahn, M.E. 2005. The Death Toll from Natural Disasters: The Role of Income, Geography, and Institutions. *Review of Economics and Statistics* 87 (2): 271–284.

Kirzner, I.M. 1985. The Perils of Regulation: A Market-Process Perspective. In *Discovery and the Capitalist Process*. Chicago, IL: The University of Chicago Press.

Knabb, R.D., J.R. Rhome, and D.P. Brown. 2006. *Tropical Cyclone Report: Hurricane Katrina, 23–20 August 2005*. National Hurricane Center. Accessed August 10, 2006. http://www.nhc.noaa.gov/data/tcr/AL122005_Katrina.pdf.

Lavoie, D. 1985a. *Rivalry and Central Planning: The Socialist Calculation Debate Revisited*. New York: Cambridge University Press.

———. 1985b. *National Economic Planning: What Is Left?* Washington, DC: Cato Institute.

Leeson, P.T. 2014. *Anarchy Unbound: Why Self-Governance Works Better than You Think*. New York: Cambridge University Press.

Mill, J.S. [1848] 1885. *Principles of Political Economy*. New York: D. Appleton and Company.

Mises, L. [1920] 1990. *Economic Calculation in the Socialist Commonwealth*. Auburn, AL: Mises Institute.

Murtazashvili, J. 2016. *Informal Order and the State in Afghanistan*. New York: Cambridge University Press.

Norris, F.H., J.L. Perilla, J.K. Riad, K. Kaniasty, and E.A. Lavizzo. 1999. Stability and Change in Stress, Resources, and Psychological Distress Following Natural Disaster: Findings from Hurricane Andrew. *Anxiety, Stress & Coping* 12 (4): 363–396.

Paton, D. 2007. Preparing for Natural Hazards: The Role of Community Trust. *Disaster Prevention and Management: An International Journal* 16 (3): 370–379.

Peacock, W.G. 2003. Hurricane Mitigation Status and Factors Influencing Mitigation Status Among Florida's Single-Family Homeowners. *Natural Hazards Review* 4 (3): 149–158.

Peek, L. 2008. Children and Disasters: Understanding Vulnerability, Developing Capacities, and Promoting Resilience. *Children, Youth, and Environments* 18: 1–29.

Pipa, T. 2006. *Weathering the Storm: The Role of Local Nonprofits in the Hurricane Katrina Relief Effort.* Nonprofit Sector Research Fund. Aspen Institute.

Shaw, R., and K. Goda. 2004. From Disaster to Sustainable Civil Society: The Kobe Experience. *Disasters* 28 (1): 16–40.

Sobel, R.S., and P.T. Leeson. 2007. The Use of Knowledge in Natural-Disaster Relief Management. *The Independent Review* 11 (4): 519–532.

Springer, C.G. 2009. Emergency Managers as Change Agents. *Ideas from an Emerging Field: Teaching Emergency Management in Higher Education* 12 (1): 197–211.

Storr, V.H., S. Haeffele-Balch, and L.E. Grube. 2015. *Community Revival in the Wake of Disaster: Lessons in Local Entrepreneurship.* New York: Palgrave Macmillan.

———. 2017. Social Capital and Social Learning after Hurricane Sandy. *The Review of Austrian Economics* 30 (4): 447–467.

Thaler, R., and C. Sunstein. 2008. *Nudge: Improving Decisions About Health, Wealth and Happiness.* New York: Penguin Press.

Tierney, K.J. 2007. Testimony on Needed Emergency Management Reforms. *Journal of Homeland Security and Emergency Management* 4 (3): 15.

Wisner, B., P. Blaikie, T. Cannon, and I. Davis. 2004. *At Risk: Natural Hazards, People's Vulnerability, and Disasters.* 2nd ed. New York: Routledge.

Wright, J.D. 1979. *After the Clean-Up: Long Range Effects of Natural Disasters.* Beverly Hills: Sage Publications.

2

The *What, How,* and *Why* of Bottom-Up Rebuilding and Recovery After Natural Disasters

Laura E. Grube

2.1 Introduction

In the United States, The Stafford Act (enacted in 1988 and amended in 2016) establishes the current system of federal disaster assistance in which a presidential disaster declaration triggers assistance provided by the Federal Emergency Management Agency (FEMA).[1] In 2017 alone, there were 69 declared disasters, including Hurricane Harvey and wildfires in California. Total federal spending in response to the 2017 disasters was approximately $130 billion.[2]

With dozens of presidential declarations each year and federal spending on natural disasters in the hundreds of billions, it is easy to understand how disaster relief in the United States is almost synonymous with FEMA and federal government. Federal disaster response, however, is a relatively new phenomenon in U.S. history. Until well into the twentieth century, disaster relief was primarily provided through bottom-up efforts.

L. E. Grube (✉)
Department of Economics, Beloit College, Beloit, WI, USA
e-mail: grubel@beloit.edu

© The Author(s) 2020
S. Haeffele, V. H. Storr (eds.), *Bottom-up Responses to Crisis*, Mercatus Studies
in Political and Social Economy, https://doi.org/10.1007/978-3-030-39312-0_2

Skarbek (2014, 160), for example, explains how the Chicago Relief and Aid Society, a bottom-up relief effort, took action following the Chicago Fire in 1871, which damaged approximately 17,000 buildings, resulted in over 300 deaths, and left 300,000 city residents homeless. The organization, in coordination with other civil society groups, distributed food and supplies to victims and raised money for assistance efforts. Indeed, similar responses took place after disasters around the country. A dramatic change came following the two world wars, when disaster response was subsumed under civil defense efforts and was also carried out by New Deal agencies (see Roberts 2013).

Bottom-up responses are still critical to post-disaster rebuilding and recovery. Take, for example, The Cajun Navy, a group organized after 2005 Hurricane Katrina, that donates their boats and labor to help victims of flooding.[3] Or, the restaurant owner who works overtime and uses his social network to get his restaurant back up and running and provide food to the residents who have returned and the contractors who are busy repairing and rebuilding homes and businesses. Bottom-up responses are actions organized and driven by the local communities affected. They may be for profit, or not-for-profit. Bottom-up responses take place alongside federal government response to disaster.

A growing literature suggests that bottom-up responses can be effective in the process of rebuilding and recovery post-disaster (Aldrich 2012; Beggs et al. 1996; Chamlee-Wright 2010). Local actors and organizations, including commercial entrepreneurs, can supply needed goods, services, and information (Storr et al. 2015). Bottom-up efforts have access to knowledge about what is needed, who might require assistance, and what resources already exist within the impacted community. Social capital, or social networks, are important tools that help bottom-up efforts distribute assistance. Local actors also signal to others that the community is coming back, and therefore, encourage rebuilding and recovery (Storr et al. 2015). And, importantly, local actors provide emotional support and strength during a time when individuals are overwhelmed.

In this chapter, I summarize the arguments for community-based efforts to rebuild and recover following disasters. I focus on rebuilding and recovery, rather than immediate response. I do this for two reasons.

First, there are strong reasons to believe that local actors encourage rebuilding and recovery in a way that outsiders (e.g. FEMA) cannot. Second, the empirical evidence that I have available focuses primarily on rebuilding and recovery.

I organize the arguments into *what* community actors can do following disaster, *how* bottom-up efforts are active in rebuilding and recovery, and *why* individuals rely on bottom-up efforts. Then, I present two case studies. The first case study examines the Bayswater community on the Rockaway Peninsula in New York in the aftermath of Hurricane Sandy in 2012. The second case study focuses on the Broadmoor neighborhood in New Orleans, Louisiana after Hurricane Katrina in 2005. Next, I outline a few policies that allow for community actors to engage in rebuilding and recovery and then conclude.

2.2 The *What, How,* and *Why* of Bottom-Up Responses to Disasters

2.2.1 *What* Bottom-Up Efforts Can Do

Bottom-up efforts can provide needed goods and services in the post-disaster environment. The type of assistance and scale of assistance will be impacted, in part, by the particular disaster (i.e. What is the level of damage? How widespread is the damage?). Evidence from natural disasters such as Hurricane Katrina (2005) and Hurricane Sandy (2012) suggest that community organizations, for example, can solicit donations of money or goods and services and distribute these to individuals impacted by disaster. Churches and other civic organizations can lead clean-up efforts, make food and hot meals available, and locate places for people to stay. Further, local actors and organizations can get important goods, services, and information (including information about assistance, who is planning to return, and how to go about the rebuilding process) to individuals and families in their communities.

Bottom-up efforts can both (1) provide needed goods, services, and information, and importantly, (2) can coordinate rebuilding and recovery.

A large literature documents the efforts of social entrepreneurs and non-profit organizations in the post-disaster context. Shaw and Goda (2004), for example, describe how a variety of non-profit organizations formed before the Kobe earthquake (in Kobe, Japan) had established systems of mutual support that were then effectively leveraged in the aftermath of the earthquake. Bolin and Stanford (1998) describe how non-governmental organizations stepped in to provide additional support to vulnerable populations, including low-income individuals, Latinos, and farm workers following the 1994 earthquake in Northridge, California. Storr et al. (2015) and Grube and Storr (2018) have written on the role of commercial entrepreneurs, important actors in bottom-up efforts, in rebuilding and recovery. Commercial entrepreneurs can donate time and effort, but perhaps even more importantly, by working to rebuild their own businesses, they contribute to recovery. If entrepreneurs can reopen a construction business, grocery store, or home goods shop, those in the community can make use of those goods and services. For example, Storr et al. (2015) describe how Mike Dean* reopened his grocery store in Central City 6 months after Hurricane Katrina.[4] His business offered premade meals and an ATM and fax machine (Storr et al. 2015, 117–118). Dean noted that day laborers would gather at his store for breakfast and lunch as it was one of the few places to offer a hot meal. The store also made it easier for residents to return because they could use the fax machine to submit private insurance claims or forms for FEMA assistance.

In addition, community actors may be able to *coordinate* rebuilding and recovery efforts. In the post-disaster context (as in mundane times) some exchanges occur in the market context and are guided by prices and profit and loss, and other exchanges take place outside the market. Scholars have advanced our theoretical understanding of how individuals engage in decision-making in non-priced environments (Chamlee-Wright and Myers 2008; Smith and Sutter 2017). Whether in a market (where goods are for sale) or outside the market (where goods are donated), coordination requires (a) the right combination of goods, services, and information so that people can engage in clean-up efforts and begin the rebuilding process. Community actors may become aware that daycare help is needed so that parents can focus on sorting through their damaged homes, or that ready-to-eat meals are necessary for people who are driving in and working on their homes during daylight hours. And, (b) getting these items to those who demand them is as important. Knowing who has returned and how to reach them requires the knowledge of community actors. Further, if individuals have (c) access to some sort of feedback mechanism, they can be more certain that their efforts are appropriate.

Finally, the actions of bottom-up efforts serve as signals that aid widespread coordination (across large swaths of a neighborhood) and recovery. When local actors are active in rebuilding and are visible in the community speaking to neighbors, organizing community events, or even lobbying city or state government, these actions show a credible commitment to rebuilding. As Chamlee-Wright and Storr (2009a) explain, bottom-up efforts can increase the probability that others will return (by actively reaching out to displaced residents) and raise the expected value of return (i.e. increase the benefit, by rebuilding churches, key businesses, and other community amenities). Bottom-up efforts provide a signal that is incorporated into the decision-making of others and contributes to recovery.

2.2.2 *How* Bottom-Up Efforts Respond and Aid in Recovery

Bottom-up efforts are able to provide needed goods and services and coordinate rebuilding and recovery because (1) of their access to local knowledge, (2) ability to use social capital (i.e. social networks), and (3) their flexibility (see Chamlee-Wright 2010; Coyne and Lemke 2012; Storr et al. 2015). Because bottom-up efforts operate on the ground, come from the communities impacted, and are generally decentralized, they have access to local knowledge (Hayek 1945). Relevant local knowledge may be related to what resources—for example, boats, available buildings, or people with particular skills—exist in the community and may be leveraged. It may also include knowledge of changing circumstances and therefore changing needs. It may be information about the particular preferences of the community (tied to ethnicity, or religious beliefs) that may be relevant for food donations or making temporary shelter available.

Social capital (here used to describe social networks) is critical infrastructure to make use of local knowledge and distribute goods and services. The owner of the corner grocery store, for example, may observe that people need rubber gloves, bleach, and other cleaning supplies, and he may rely on his suppliers and friends in the wholesale business to obtain the items for his store. Or, someone may have an extra bedroom that they would like to make available for someone else in need, and they may reach out to contacts within their church to locate a dormer. Within the post-disaster literature, scholars have described how different types of social capital are leveraged. There are three different types of social capital—bonding, bridging, and linking—which refer to the strength of the connection and whether the connection is across a like or unlike group (Woolcock 2001). Bonding social capital, or strong ties between like actors (e.g. the connections within a family), are a key source of informal disaster assistance (Hurlbert, Haines, et al. 2000; Hurlbert, Beggs, et al. 2001; Chamlee-Wright and Storr 2009a). Bridging or linking social capital, which describes weaker ties across more varied groups, can be a valuable source of information because the ties exist across different geographical areas and socio-economic classes (e.g. think of the owner of the corner grocery store who needs supplies).

Another advantage of such bottom-up efforts is that they offer flexibility. This flexibility comes about in two ways. First, they are less constrained than centralized efforts that may require individual actors to follow specific rules or protocols. Instead, bottom-up efforts generally support adaptation to changing circumstances. Second, flexibility comes in the form of scalability: bottom-up efforts may be able to coordinate with others to increase the amount of assistance or decrease the amount of assistance (Coyne and Lemke 2012). For example, a single church may be able to provide lunches for a few dozen people; however, if more lunches are needed, they may partner with other area churches or organizations. Again, this flexibility is in contrast to federal government efforts, which cannot easily offer small-scale provision of goods and services.

2.2.3   *Why* Individuals Leverage Bottom-Up Efforts

The question of why individuals rely on bottom-up efforts (e.g. in contrast to formal assistance through insurance or government programs) is tied to the systems that operate during mundane times and what resources are "on-hand" (Grube and Storr 2014). During mundane times individuals rely on commercial businesses for needed goods and services; they turn to a civic organization, neighborhood group, or church in certain times of need; and they reach out to family and close friends for last minute child care, assistance with a house project, or help moving. It makes sense then that these same structures would be activated following a disaster. These are resources that individuals know about and that are trustworthy.

Within the literature on entrepreneurship, using the resources "on hand" is referred to as bricolage. As Di Domenico et al. (2010, 685) explain, "bricolage has been used to denote resourcefulness and adaptability within an existing context." Johannisson and Olaison (2007) refer to social bricolage as they describe the response to Hurricane Gudrun (2005) in southern Sweden. Even when emergency plans exist, responding to disaster always involves some level of spontaneity, which is why the authors explain, residents relied on their social networks and resources available.

Also important, bottom-up efforts, because they are led by local residents, business owners, and members of civil society organizations, are sources that may provide emotional support during a time when individuals are feeling overwhelmed. Bottom-up efforts may include a familiar face, and someone who is going through a similar ordeal. Chamlee-Wright and Storr (2009b) note that residents as well as church members and community organizations in the Ninth Ward after Hurricane Katrina held to fond memories of the neighborhood—a place where people attended PTA meetings, things were "relaxed," and residents got together for barbecues and block parties—and shared these memories with each other. In addition to sharing positive memories, bottom-up efforts may use common stories of perseverance to motivate themselves and others around rebuilding and recovery. For example,

Chamlee-Wright (2018, 470) describes how St. Bernard Parish resident, Michael Fontana* described his community and its residents after Hurricane Katrina,

> We in the Parish, we are a self-sufficient type of community. We all work … we're a blue-collar community—we're not afraid of work … we realized that, "look, we got where we were, and we're the only ones that are gonna restore where we were."

Individuals may reach out to community actors for assistance, then, not only because they are aware of them as resources but also because they know they will provide reassurance, a reminder of why their neighborhood is so special, and motivation to do the hard work of rebuilding and recovery.

2.3   Case Studies of Bottom-Up Efforts Following Disasters

In-depth interviews are an especially useful method for understanding how people engage in rebuilding and recovery. In the aftermath of Hurricane Katrina (2005), a team of scholars and researchers with the Mercatus Center (a research center affiliated with George Mason University) traveled to New Orleans, LA to study community response to disaster.[5] The scholars and researchers interviewed over 350 residents, business owners, and members of community organizations. Following Hurricane Sandy (2012), a smaller team of scholars interviewed residents and members of community organizations to learn about rebuilding and recovery efforts on the Rockaway Peninsula in New York. In total, 16 interviews were completed.

Below, I highlight two communities, Bayswater in New York City and Broadmoor in New Orleans. I selected these two cases because they present very different communities in terms of the level of diversity within the community and the type of social capital, or networks, found in the community. The post-disaster literature offers examples of both types of communities—described as heterogeneous, loosely connected versus homogeneous, tightly knit—being able to effectively respond to disaster. There is more literature, however, that supports the hypothesis that homogeneous, tightly knit communities will be able to effectively respond to disaster using the logic that individuals in these communities (1) know what to expect of others in the community and (2) may be able to rely on club goods provided (e.g. church funds, or other types of assistance) (Aldrich 2011a, b; Hurlbert, Haines, et al. 2000; Hurlbert, Beggs, et al. 2001; Chamlee-Wright and Storr 2009a; Storr and Haeffele-Balch 2012). I present Bayswater in New York City first as an example of a homogeneous, tightly knit community. Broadmoor in New Orleans (a more heterogeneous, loosely connect community) is the "hard case," or scenario where we might suspect that rebuilding and recovery would be more challenging. Notably, the damage sustained in Broadmoor after Hurricane Katrina is also more significant than the damage sustained in Bayswater after Hurricane Sandy. In both cases collective action does take place, and we see rebuilding and recovery.

2.3.1   Bottom-Up Assistance in the Orthodox Jewish Community, Bayswater, New York[6]

Hurricane Sandy hit the East Coast of the United States in October of 2012. In the United States, 73 people were killed. In New York City alone, 305,000 homes were destroyed or damaged. Estimated total property damage in the United States was $60 billion.

Bayswater is on the Rockaway Peninsula in the borough of Queens in New York City. The community experienced as much as six feet of flooding as a result of the storm surge, and much of the neighborhood was without power for several weeks. There is a large Orthodox Jewish community in Bayswater, and there are eight Jewish synagogues. Before Hurricane Sandy and in the aftermath of the storm, the Jewish community and the synagogues worked to meet the needs of the community.

Storr et al. (2015) have written on how various individuals, synagogues, and community organizations on the Rockaway Peninsula responded to Hurricane Sandy. For example, the authors highlight the efforts of Rabbi Mordechai Kruger, a longtime resident of Bayswater, a rabbi at the Agudas Yisroel of Bayswater synagogue, and the founder of the Bayswater Neighbor's Fund. Prior to Hurricane Sandy, Rabbi Kruger had established the Bayswater Neighbor's Fund to provide short-term help to those in need. He relied on local knowledge through community contacts to identify people who were struggling, and people in the community gave donations, trusting Rabbi Kruger to distribute the funds responsibly. In addition, Rabbi Kruger worked as a caseworker for the Metropolitan Council on Jewish Poverty (Met Council) and counseled Jewish adults on career goals and professional training.

Rabbi Kruger's experience in social services made him a logical leader in post-disaster assistance following Hurricane Sandy. Another Jewish organization, Achiezer (Hebrew for "helping a brother"), reinstated a community assistance fund (CAF) that had been created after the Great Recession (2008). The fund enlisted the help of trusted members of the community to locate those who had lost household items (including appliances, beds, and clothing) and sustained damage to their homes and encourage them to apply for assistance. Rabbi Kruger became the representative of CAF for Bayswater.

Rabbi Kruger visited with people who had assembled at a local community organization, went door-to-door, and asked others to help spread the word about CAF. In order to ensure that particular needs were met, Rabbi Kruger and others documented damages in a spreadsheet. This helped direct donated items to those who needed them. It also provided helpful information to respond to inquiries about what was needed. In total over $11 million was donated to CAF and 1000 families received assistance.

2.3.2   The Broadmoor Improvement Association in Broadmoor, New Orleans[7]

Hurricane Katrina hit the United States in August of 2005, affecting four states, Louisiana, Mississippi, Alabama, and the southern tip of Florida. Over 1800 people died as a result of the hurricane and subsequent flooding. New Orleans, Louisiana sustained the worst damage. Over 80 percent of the city was flooded, and 134,000 housing units were damaged.

Broadmoor is located just west of downtown and east of Tulane University. The neighborhood has been described as a microcosm of the larger New Orleans. Before Katrina, median household income was $27,000 and the racial and ethnic makeup of the neighborhood was 68 percent African American, 26 percent white, and approximately 4 percent Hispanic or Latino (2000 U.S. Census). Broadmoor had, on average, flood waters of eight feet, meaning that if structures were not elevated, first floor living spaces were destroyed.

Storr and Haeffele-Balch (2012) as well as Storr et al. (2015) have written about the role of the Broadmoor Improvement Association (BIA) in recovery and rebuilding efforts. Prior to Katrina, the BIA, which was established in the 1930s, offered a forum to discuss and lobby for public services and infrastructure, implemented community-organized efforts such as a neighborhood watch program, and in the 1970s, fought against "blockbusting," a practice which encouraged the racial separation of neighborhoods (Storr and Haeffele-Balch 2012, 305). After Katrina, the City had designated Broadmoor as an area that would not be rebuilt (indicated by a green dot on City redevelopment plans).

Given the activities of BIA before Katrina, it is unsurprising that the organization would be active in rebuilding and recovery efforts. The President of BIA, LaToya Cantrell, sprang into action.[8] The association used existing neighborhood records and member lists to contact residents via text messages, emails, phone calls, and flyers and encouraged them to return. Being able to access member lists with contact information allowed the group to coordinate return in a way that would have been difficult without the established records and connections.

In their efforts to coordinate return, leaders of the BIA realized that the community had a wealth of resources. As Maggie Carrol, secretary of the BIA, explained, people came forward and brought their skills in marketing and fundraising. The organization leveraged local knowledge, resources that were on hand, and received support from a number of media outlets, philanthropic organizations, and a research center. Broadmoor's story was told in the New Orleans *Times-Picayune, National Public Radio,* and Delta Airlines' *Delta Sky* magazine. In addition, the community received support from the Clinton Global Initiative, the Carnegie Corporation of New York, Mercy Corps, and the Belfer Center for Science and International Affairs at Harvard University's Kennedy School of Government.

Through the efforts of the BIA, the community was able to show viability (that at least 50 percent of residents were committed to return) and successfully rebound from Hurricane Katrina. Prior to Hurricane Katrina, the population of Broadmoor was 9119 people. Two years later, the population was 5251 (58 percent pre-storm population). Five years later, in 2010, the population was 6359 (70 percent pre-storm population).[9]

2.4   Policies That Promote Bottom-Up Efforts

Bottom-up efforts have the potential to respond to crisis. Bottom-up efforts, in most contexts and certainly in the context of the United States, operate alongside government efforts to respond to disaster. FEMA has recognized the importance of bottom-up efforts, as evidenced by concepts such as the Whole Community Approach, that emphasizes the need for a variety of stakeholders to work together.

There are other ways that the policy environment can encourage bottom-up responses and create an enabling environment. Specifically, government can:

1. Ensure that rules are clear and known in advance;
2. Protect private property; and
3. Allow community actors to step in.

Government can ensure that, for example, residents and business owners know when they will be allowed back to their properties, what the requirements are for rebuilding, and what assistance is available, as well as who qualifies and how to apply. When these rules are clear and known in advance, people understand what steps they need to take to begin rebuilding, and they can prioritize and plan when they will do various tasks. For example, if a building permit is required, but the process is straightforward (and relatively fast), a business owner can start to rebuild quickly. If rebuilding rules are similarly clear, then she has less risk of needing to start over and redo work that she had already completed.

By protecting private property, governments also encourage rebuilding and recovery. If residents feel uncertain about their property rights, they will be less likely to rebuild or make investments to their property. After a disaster, local governments may designate certain areas with a green dot, indicating that they may not be allowed to rebuild (and instead, the land will be converted into green space). Eminent domain is used to take properties. Beito and Smith (2012) describe how Joplin, MO was able to rebound relatively quickly following a devastating tornado in 2011. Tuscaloosa, AL, which was also destroyed by a tornado in the same year, engaged in a large-scale redevelopment of the downtown business district. Not knowing if or when they would reopen, many businesses opted to move elsewhere. Uncertainties around property contributed to a much slower recovery in Tuscaloosa.

Immediately following a disaster some residents may be prohibited from returning to their homes. Local governments should minimize this period. When residents are allowed to return, local governments should take steps to reduce the costs of rebuilding, such as relax occupational licensing rules (at a minimum, allowing tradespeople who are licensed in other states to do work) and ease the process for obtaining building permits. Local actors drive rebuilding and recovery and allowing them to begin their work helps to ensure a faster recovery.

2.5   Conclusion

Community-based responses to disasters are critical for community rebuilding and recovery. These bottom-up efforts can provide the needed goods, services, and information and can coordinate rebuilding and recovery. Bottom-up efforts benefit from access to local knowledge, the ability to use social capital, and their flexibility. There are a growing number of case studies that document local efforts to rebuild and recover after natural disaster.

If bottom-up responses are important for post-disaster rebuilding and recovery, then a major implication is that efforts should be made to allow community actors to act. Indeed, ensuring that rules are clear and known in advance and protecting private property is important.

Notes

1. See FEMA (2016).
2. Available online at https://riskcenter.wharton.upenn.edu/disaster-aid/federal-disaster-rebuilding-spending-look-numbers/.
3. See, for example, Brasted (2016).
4. This individual was interviewed as part of the Mercatus Gulf Coast Recovery Project (see Sect. 2.3 for more information on the project). Pseudonyms are denoted with an asterisk.
5. For an extended discussion of methodology, see Chamlee-Wright (2010) and Storr et al. (2015).
6. For more information on this case study, see Storr et al. (2015, 2017a, b, 2018).
7. For more information on this case study, see Storr and Haeffele-Balch (2012) and Storr et al. (2015).
8. LaToya Cantrell was elected mayor of New Orleans in 2018.
9. Data comes from the Data Center, Active Residential Addresses, available online at https://www.datacenterresearch.org/data-resources/active-addresses-by-zip-code/ (accessed May 14, 2018).

References

Aldrich, D. 2011a. The Externalities of Social Capital: Post-Tsunami Recovery in Southeast India. *Journal of Civil Society* 8 (1): 81–99.

———. 2011b. The Power of People: Social Capital's Role in Recovery from the 1995 Kobe Earthquake. *Natural Hazards* 56 (3): 595–611.

———. 2012. *Building Resilience Social Capital in Post-Disaster Recovery*. Chicago: University of Chicago Press.

Beggs, J.J., V.A. Haines, and J.S. Hurlbert. 1996. Situational Contingencies Surrounding the Receipt of Informal Support. *Social Forces* 75 (1): 201–222.

Beito, D., and D. Smith. 2012. Tornado Recovery: How Joplin Is Beating Tuscaloosa. *Wall Street Journal*, April 13. https://www.wsj.com/articles/SB10001424052702303404704577309220933715082.

Bolin, R., and L. Stanford. 1998. The Northridge Earthquake: Community-Based Approaches to Unmet Recovery Needs. *Disasters* 22 (1): 21–38.

Brasted, C. 2016. New Orleanians Join Cajun Navy: 'It Can Get Treacherous Real Quick.' *NOLA.com*, August 16. http://www.nola.com/weather/index. ssf/2016/08/cajun_navy_louisiana_floods_re.html.

Chamlee-Wright, E. 2010. *The Cultural and Political Economy of Recovery*. New York: Routledge.

———. 2018. The Power of Narrative in Post-Disaster Entrepreneurial Response. *The Review of Austrian Economics* 31 (4): 467–472.

Chamlee-Wright, E., and J. Myers. 2008. Discovery and Social Learning in Non-Priced Environments: An Austrian View of Social Network Theory. *The Review of Austrian Economics* 21: 151–166.

Chamlee-Wright, E., and V.H. Storr. 2009a. Club Goods and Post-Disaster Community Return. *Rationality and Society* 21 (4): 429–458.

———. 2009b. There's No Place Like New Orleans: Sense of Place and Community Recovery in the Ninth Ward After Hurricane Katrina. *Journal of Urban Affairs* 31 (5): 615–634.

Coyne, C.J., and J.S. Lemke. 2012. Lessons from *The Cultural and Political Economy of Recovery*. *American Journal of Economics and Sociology* 71 (1): 215–228.

Di Domenico, M.L., H. Haugh, and P. Tracey. 2010. Social Bricolage: Theorizing Social Value Creation in Social Enterprises. *Entrepreneurship Theory and Practice* 34 (4): 681–703.

FEMA. 2016. *Robert T. Stafford Disaster Relief and Emergency Assistance Act, as Amended, and Related Authorities as of August 2016, Public Law 93–288*. Washington, DC: Federal Emergency Management Agency and US Congress. https://www.fema.gov/media-library/assets/documents/15271.

Grube, L.E., and V.H. Storr. 2014. The Capacity for Self-Governance and Post-Disaster Resiliency. *The Review of Austrian Economics* 27 (3): 301–324.

———. 2018. Embedded Entrepreneurs and Post-Disaster Recovery. *Entrepreneurship and Regional Development* 30 (7–8): 800–821.

Hayek, F.A. 1945. The Use of Knowledge in Society. *The American Economic Review* 35 (4): 519–530.

Hurlbert, J., V. Haines, and J. Beggs. 2000. Core Networks and Tie Activation: What Kinds of Routine Networks Allocate Resources in Nonroutine Situations? *American Sociological Review* 65 (4): 598–618.

Hurlbert, J., J. Beggs, and V. Haines. 2001. Social Capital in Extreme Environments. In *Social Capital: Theory and Research*, ed. N. Lin, K. Cook, and R. Burt. New York: Aldine De Gruyter.

Johannisson, B., and L. Olaison. 2007. The Moment of Truth—Reconstructing Entrepreneurship and Social Capital in the Eye of the Storm. *Review of Social Economy* 65 (1): 55–78.

Roberts, P. 2013. *Disasters and the American State: How Politicians, Bureaucrats, and the Public Prepare for the Unexpected.* Cambridge: Cambridge University Press.

Shaw, R., and K. Goda. 2004. From Disaster to Sustainable Civil Society: The Kobe Experience. *Disasters* 28 (1): 16–40.

Skarbek, E. 2014. The Chicago Fire of 1871: A Bottom-Up Approach to Disaster Relief. *Public Choice* 160 (1–2): 155–180.

Smith, D., and D. Sutter. 2017. Coordination in Disaster: Nonprice Learning and the Allocation of Resources After Disaster. *The Review of Austrian Economics* 30 (4): 469–492.

Storr, V.H., and S. Haeffele-Balch. 2012. Post-Disaster Community Recovery in Heterogeneous, Loosely Connected Communities. *Review of Social Economy* 70 (3): 295–314.

Storr, V.H., S. Haeffele-Balch, and L.E. Grube. 2015. *Community Revival in the Wake of Disaster Lessons in Local Entrepreneurship.* New York: Palgrave Macmillan.

Storr, V.H., L.E. Grube, and S. Haeffele-Balch. 2017a. Polycentric Orders and Post-Disaster Recovery: A Case Study of One Orthodox Jewish Community Following Hurricane Sandy. *The Journal of Institutional Economics* 13 (4): 875–897.

Storr, V.H., S. Haeffele-Balch, and L.E. Grube. 2017b. Social Capital and Social Learning After Hurricane Sandy. *The Review of Austrian Economics* 30 (4): 447–467.

———. 2018. Entrepreneurs Drive Community Revival in the Wake of Disasters. *The Review of Austrian Economics* 31 (4): 479–484.

Woolcock, M. 2001. The Place of Social Capital in Understanding Social and Economic Outcomes. *Canadian Journal of Policy Research* 2 (1): 11–17.

3

Nonviolent Action

Joshua Ammons and Christopher J. Coyne

3.1 Introduction

Nonviolent action entails exerting power to bring about change through means which avoid the use of physical force. Examples of nonviolent action include protests, boycotts, civil disobedience, and noncooperation, among others. Although it is possible for a single individual to engage in nonviolence, large-scale efforts, which involve numerous people working together to achieve some shared goal, are associated with broader societal change. Historically, these goals have included undermining authoritarian governments; contesting injustices; preserving

J. Ammons
Department of Economics, George Mason University, Fairfax, VA, USA
e-mail: Jammons@ihs.gmu.edu

C. J. Coyne (✉)
Department of Economics, George Mason University, Fairfax, VA, USA

F. A. Hayek Program for Advanced Study in Philosophy, Politics, and
Economics, Mercatus Center at George Mason University, Fairfax, VA, USA
e-mail: ccoyne3@gmu.edu

29

S. Haeffele, V. H. Storr (eds.), *Bottom-up Responses to Crisis*, Mercatus Studies
in Political and Social Economy, https://doi.org/10.1007/978-3-030-39312-0_3

human rights, freedoms, and civil liberties; preventing coups d'état; defending against external threats; and expelling foreign invaders, among others.[1]

Nonviolent action can be understood as a type of bottom-up response to a crisis of illegitimacy. For example, nonviolent action that seeks to combat a foreign invasion or a coup d'état is based on the idea that these acts represent illegitimate uses of force. These illegitimate acts create a crisis by threatening society's institutions and the ways of life of those living within those institutions. Those threatened by the crisis can respond in one of three ways. They can acquiesce and accept the change, which would have a legitimizing effect. They can reject the change as illegitimate and combat it through violence. Or, they can reject the change as illegitimate and combat it through nonviolence.

This example highlights four salient features of nonviolent action. First, nonviolent action is a response to perceived illegitimacy. This illegitimacy can come from a variety of sources—external and internal violent threats, injustices against segments, or the entirety, of the population, etc. While nonviolent action may be perceived as the source of disruption to the order of society, it is in fact a response to some pre-existing threat to order. Second, nonviolent action is distinct from violent action. By definition, nonviolence excludes the use of physical force. Third, nonviolent action is not passive inaction. Instead, it is pro-active in that it involves people taking steps to bring about change in the face of perceived illegitimacy. Fourth, nonviolent action involves collective action on the part of a segment of the population that joins together in a common cause to fight a perceived illegitimacy. The group must find ways to cooperate and coordinate while maintaining a shared commitment to refraining from engaging in violence.

The specifics of nonviolent action vary across contexts. In some cases, nonviolent action seeks to change the overarching institutions which govern society. In other cases, nonviolent action is a method for bringing about policy changes within an existing set of overarching institutions which remain in place. While the specific manifestation of nonviolent action will vary, the four features of nonviolent action apply across cases.

The purpose of this chapter is to provide an overview of the key thinkers, practitioners, and writings on nonviolent action. Our purpose is twofold. First, we aim to introduce readers to the key figures in the long tradition of nonviolent action. Second, we seek to emphasize nonviolent action as an important means for responding to crises. This approach is bottom-up in that it requires people figuring out ways to work together collectively to generate change to the status quo without a single, over-arching entity directing the effort.

We proceed as follows. Section 3.2 discusses those who contributed to our understanding of nonviolent action during the pre-nineteenth century (Sect. 3.2.1) and nineteenth and early twentieth centuries (Sect. 3.2.2). Section 3.3 reviews the work of Gene Sharp, the preeminent theorist of nonviolent resistance during the late twentieth century. Section 3.4 discusses contemporary work on nonviolent action. Section 3.5 concludes with areas for future research.

3.2   Early Thinkers and Practitioners

3.2.1   Pre-Nineteenth Century

The writings of Étienne de La Boétie are among the first philosophical treatments of nonviolent action. La Boétie ([1735] 1942) altered perceptions of political power stating that political authority derives from the consent of the governed. Explicit in his observation is the idea that widespread withdrawal of consent was sufficient for undermining government power. Withdrawal from military service and taxation were two of the primary methods he advocated to starve the state of the resources necessary to carry out its activities. Without these resources, he argued, rulers lacked the power to impose their will on the masses. The idea that government is fragile and dependent on a compliant populous ran counter to the Divine Right of Kings which was commonly accepted at the time.

During the 1700s in America, Benjamin Lay, a radical Quaker abolitionist, was an early practitioner of nonviolent action, employing public speeches, dramatic performances, and political writings (Rediker 2017). Lay challenged the orthodoxy of slavery and, in doing so, was one of the most successful practitioners of nonviolent action in the 1700s. Speaking truth to power, Lay sought to change the ideology that undergirded the institution of slavery. Through carefully planned campaigns, he sought to persuade passive supporters of slavery of the institution's inherent injustice. Well after his death in 1759, Lay's efforts continued to influence the ideology of Quakers, who worked to end slavery in the United States and Britain.

3.2.2   The Nineteenth and Early Twentieth Centuries

William Lloyd Garrison, the radical abolitionist, and proponent of women's rights, believed that withdrawing consent from the government through civil disobedience was crucial for achieving political reform (Crosby 1905; Dillon 1974). Garrison was of the belief that suitable social change required a fundamental ideological shift (Kraditor 1989). His objection to the Civil War was puzzling to many abolitionists, but at the heart of his objection was a plea for nonviolent action as a means for bringing about change (Brock 1968). He proposed, and employed, a variety of nonviolent methods including formal statements, communications with wider audiences, public assemblies, social noncooperation, and political noncooperation.

Henry David Thoreau, a contemporary of Garrison, was a nineteenth-century tax resistor, prisoner, and abolitionist, who practiced civil disobedience (Thoreau 1963). Instead of participating in politics, Thoreau used acts of nonviolence such as the withholding of taxes, public speeches, writing, and participation in the Underground Railroad to fight the institution of slavery (Bedau 1969). Thoreau's classic essay on civil disobedience emphasized limited government and the primacy of individual conscious (Thoreau 1969). Breaking the law, he argued, was necessary to have a clear conscience and to correct unjust laws. Thoreau's essay on civil disobedience influenced Mahatma Gandhi (Bhattacharya 1977; Hunt 1986), Leo Tolstoy (Manning 1943), Frank Chodorov (1980), and Martin Luther King (Oates 1994), among others.

Tolstoy's objections to the Russian government's power and use of violence derived primarily from moral conviction (Tolstoy 1885). Christian pacifism, he believed, demanded a rejection of all forms of government violence including military service and domestic security forces (Tolstoy 2012). In his view, government power derived from intimidation, nationalist propaganda, religious propaganda, taxation, bribes, asset forfeiture, and equipping citizens to use violent sanctions on behalf of the state. A commitment to consistent nonviolence was, in his view, a means for combatting the evils of government power and violence. His writings inspired future writers and practitioners of nonviolent action, including Mahatma Gandhi (Nāga 1950).

Gandhi was a political strategist who prioritized nonviolent action, which he called Satyagraha (Gandhi 1993; Mattaini 2013). Though the British commanded the greatest military might in the world, the Indian people liberated themselves through nonviolent tactics. For example, the Indian Salt March supported tax evasion. During the Salt March, Gandhi's arrest increased support for the movement and diminished the popularity of the British forces. Indian civil resistance ultimately led to the end of British colonial rule (Carter 1995). After Gandhi's death, scores of academics and practitioners studied his tactics. For example, Gene Sharp (1960, 1961, 1979) wrote three books on Gandhi which provide a detailed analysis of the civil resistance movement in India with particular focus on the underlying political theory and role of nonviolent resistance tactics.

3.2.3 The Late Twentieth Century

The civil rights movement began with faith groups, many of which opposed militarism and war. A. J. Muste was a nonviolent political activist and member of the clergy who helped found the United States Fellowship of Reconciliation (FoR) (Robinson 1981). FoR began as an interfaith organization to protest the United States entry into World War I, emphasizing nonviolent alternatives. The conscientious objectors of FoR later birthed the American Civil Liberties Union (Wink 2000). Muste's writing and activism influenced civil rights and antiwar movements long after his death (Chomsky 1969).

Martin Luther King Jr. and other civil rights leaders challenged segregation in the American south using nonviolent action (King 1981).

Moral convictions motivated civil rights protesters, but they knew arguments for justice alone would not end segregation (King 2010). They viewed nonviolent action as a key ingredient in bringing about legitimate change. For example, in Nashville, James Lawson, a professor and political activist, was associated with the FoR and taught how to effectively employ nonviolent methods (Powers et al. 2011). Sit-ins, boycotts, and marches made racial discrimination costly for businesses in Nashville (Proudfoot 1962). As the economic impact of racial segregation became evident, and as the media broadcast the violence in Nashville in response to the civil rights movement, it became politically viable for Mayor Ben West to denounce segregation. This victory provided momentum for the civil rights movement, leading to broader social and political change.

Saul Alinsky believed that radicals should favor change through community organizing. His well-known book, *Rules for Radicals*, considered methods for political and institutional reform through nonviolent action (Alinsky 1989). Alinsky was instrumental in shaping social movements and change during the twentieth century. Frances Fox Piven and Richard Cloward (1979) advocated civil disobedience outside of the regular use of the existing political system. People power, as they called it, was a bottom-up method of successfully harnessing the masses to engage in protest. They emphasized individuals' great potential to change the status quo through nonviolent action which, in their view, should focus on attacking the system itself instead of seeking to work within existing institutions. Both Alinsky's (1989) and Piven and Cloward's (1979) writings remain relevant today.

3.3   Gene Sharp

Of all modern scholars studying nonviolent action, Gene Sharp is the most influential. At various times throughout his career, he was referred to as the "Clausewitz of nonviolent warfare," "the Machiavelli of nonviolence," "the dictator slayer," and "a dictator's worst nightmare." His scholarship spans a variety of topics, including the theory of power and politics, practical guides to nonviolent struggle, and civilian-based defense (Ammons and Coyne 2018).

The Politics of Nonviolent Action (1973) is Sharp's foundational text on nonviolent action. In this three-volume book, Sharp builds on La Boétie's ([1735] 1942) earlier work to articulate what he calls the "pluralistic dependency theory." According to this theory, the operations and sustainability of governments are dependent on the citizenry's goodwill, decisions, and support. Sharp identifies several sources of state power, which may be withdrawn through nonviolent action. These sources of power include (1) voluntary acceptance of authority; (2) the skills and knowledge of those who accept the ruler's authority; (3) ideological factors, such as tolerance for obedience and submission; (4) material resources, such as the ruler's control of wealth and infrastructure; and (5) sanctions which refer to the tools of control over citizens and other governments. Sharp analyzes how nonviolent methods can be used to withdraw these sources of support to weaken government power.

Throughout his research, Sharp addresses many of the misperceptions regarding violent and nonviolent action. These misperceptions include (1) that violence always works quickly, (2) that nonviolent struggle always takes very long, (3) that nonviolent struggle is weak, (4) that nonviolent struggle requires a charismatic leader, (5) that nonviolent struggle is not a cross-cultural phenomenon, (6) that nonviolent struggle requires religious beliefs, (7) that nonviolent struggle is the same as religious or ethical principled nonviolence, (8) that nonviolent struggle can only succeed against humanitarian and democratic opponents, and (9) that nonviolent struggle only succeeds by melting the hearts of the oppressors (Sharp 1970a, 1973, 2010a). In dispelling these misconceptions, Sharp demonstrates the potential effectiveness of nonviolent action and how it is often underestimated as a means of bringing about change and averting crises. As he notes, in many cases, nonviolent action can achieve goals which are typically assumed to require violence and war (Sharp 1970a).

For Sharp, successful nonviolent action is not a random event. Instead, it requires purposive coordination, training, and knowledge of the weapons of resistance. "Political jujitsu" is one such weapon, making state power a liability rather than a strength (Sharp 1973, 1990a). In this scenario violence used by the state becomes a spectacle that draws greater numbers into the opposition. If state violence is not deployed, the opposition also wins by demonstrating that civil disobedience is permissible and effective. Throughout his work, Sharp provides examples of successful nonviolent action across time and geographic space.

In the second volume of *The Politics of Nonviolent Action* (1973), Sharp compiles a list of 198 methods of nonviolent action. He stopped at 198 to indicate that the work of cataloging methods is incomplete and an ongoing project. He organizes these methods into five main categories (1) methods of nonviolent protests and persuasion—for example, public speeches, the distribution of leaflets and pamphlets, and the wearing of symbols; (2) methods of social noncooperation—for example, boycotts, suspension of social and sports activities, and withdrawing from social institutions; (3) methods of economic noncooperation—for example, economic boycotts and strikes by consumers and workers; (4) methods of political noncooperation—for example, refusing to provide public support, boycotting elections, refusing to dissolve existing, and independent institutions; and (5) methods of nonviolent intervention—for example, fasting, sit-ins, and establishing new social patterns and social institutions independent of government.

In *Social Power and Political Freedom*, Sharp (1980a) provides his most radical insights into the role of politics, civil society, and nonviolence for achieving change. He envisions a world of massive decentralization with power dispersed to local decision makers. Sharp is critical of dictatorships but also rule by unaccountable and self-interested bureaucrats who may not object to top-down commands. He cautions that democratic governments with traditional liberal democratic constitutions are subject to creeping centralization when the citizenry is indifferent to, or accepting of, government power. In this case, power can be usurped by elected officials and bureaucrats who ignore the law or make new laws to justify their narrowly interested goals. This slow, often unseen, drift into elite control occurs by officials altering the rules to become more authoritarian. Sharp argues that any society where the state is the strongest institution is subject to these potential threats. Skepticism of power is the theme that runs throughout the book, but he does not limit his discussion to the problems with concentrated power. Instead, he argues that nonviolent action may be used to provide checks on state power.

In subsequent books, Sharp (1994, 2010b, 2013) builds on his academic work to offer practical guides to engaging in nonviolent action.

These books outline practical approaches to nonviolent action for individuals living under state oppression. They are best understood as attempts to operationalize the insights Sharp developed in his prior scholarship.

Waging Nonviolent Struggle (2005) brings together and updates Sharp's previous work on nonviolent action. The volume is broken into four parts. The first part provides the theoretical foundation of nonviolent action based on his earlier writings. The second part provides numerous case studies in a variety of contexts to illustrate the nuances and workings of nonviolent action. In part three, Sharp explores the dynamics of nonviolent struggles. Finally, he discusses the move from theory to practice and considers how theory can be applied and implemented through a series of strategic planning guidelines.

As part of his broader work on nonviolent action, Sharp also focused on the idea of civilian-based defense. Civilian-based defense is a method of deterrence from internal threats (e.g., coups d'état) or foreign invasion through noncooperation or civil disobedience. This method of defense relies on the bottom-up power of civilians to ensure that internal or external forces are unable to use state power to suppress the population.

In *Making Europe Unconquerable* (1985), Sharp explains a potential defensive strategy for Europe in the wake of World War II. Instead of relying on military weapons—for example, nuclear armaments and conventional arms—Sharp argues that it is possible for European citizens to use the individual power they each possess through advanced preparation to deter and defend against internal and external threats. In *Civilian-Based Defense* (1990b), Sharp broadens these arguments beyond Europe, emphasizing that throughout history nonviolent action has been a key means of defense against both internal and foreign threats. In both books, he offers a theoretical foundation, grounded in his earlier work on nonviolent action, as well as numerous historical examples to illustrate his central thesis. Political officials in Lithuania, Latvia, and Estonia appealed to the latter book after regaining independence from the Soviet Union in 1991 (Roberts 2018).

In *The Anti-Coup* (2001), Sharp articulates how civilian-based defense can be used to thwart a coup d'état attempt or achieve the goal of regime change using nonviolent methods. Sharp believed that countries could use civilian-based defense as an alternative to military arms and violent conflict. While critics tend to compare the current state of civilian-based defense to modern military power, Sharp conveys a vision of what civilian-based defense could achieve if military resources were instead invested in civilian-based defense methods (Sharp 1980b). Among other things, Sharp emphasized how effective civilian-based defense would make it extremely difficult for an invading nation to establish political control over a territory (Sharp 1970b). For Sharp, civilian-based defense was not grounded in ideology or morality. Instead, he viewed it as a more effective means of promoting peace while limiting the devastating consequences of war and violence (Sharp 1992).

3.4 Contemporary Work on Nonviolent Action

Bleiker (1993) uses East Germany under communist rule to analyze non-violent action through the lens of Hirschman's (1970) categories of voice and exit. Hirschman argued that when an organization fails to generate adequate benefits to its members they can respond in one of two ways. They can exit by withdrawing from the relationship with the organization, or they can voice their displeasure in the hopes of bringing about change. Hirschman's analysis offers important insights into how nonviolent action might work. As Bleiker (1993) discusses, emigration out of Eastern Germany was a method of nonviolent resistance, draining the state of resources to achieve its desired ends. At the same time, he notes that voice was also fundamental to the decision of the leadership of the Socialist Unity Party of Germany (SED) to open its borders to the capitalist world. Voice manifested itself in a number of ways. For example, the Protestant church was a source of public dissent and provided a space for resistors. Newspapers, radio, films, television, and music exposed citizens to the Western lifestyle which intensified their desire to have access to other societies.

Bleiker affirms Gramsci's (2011) view that civil society is a space where ideas compete for power outside of state control. He also affirms the individualistic view of La Boétie ([1735] 1942), which grounds state power in the consent of the governed. However, Bleiker emphasizes the question that La Boétie poses: If power derives from the consent of the governed, then why does repression frequently persist? Bleiker (1993) contends that status quo bias and state propaganda propel individuals into accepting the current government and state of affairs.

Ackerman and Kruegler (1994) consider three categories of principles that make success in nonviolent action more likely. The first category includes the "principles of development" which seek to create an environment conducive to success in nonviolent action. These include the importance of (1) formulating functional objectives, (2) developing organizational strength, (3) securing access to critical resources, (4) cultivating external assistance, and (5) expanding the repertoire of nonviolent sanctions.

The second category is the "principles of engaging" which focus on maximizing the effectiveness of nonviolent action after a conflict is joined. These principles include (1) attacking the opponents' strategy for consolidating control, (2) muting the impact of the opponents' violent weapons, (3) alienating the opponents from expected bases of support, and (4) maintaining nonviolent discipline.

Finally, they offer "principles of conception" which focus on reflecting on what has been done and what can be done as the conflict continues in order to succeed. These principles include (1) assessing events and options in light of levels of strategic decision making, (2) adjusting offensive and defensive operations according to the relative vulnerabilities of the protagonist, and (3) sustaining continuity between sanctions, mechanisms, and objectives.

In developing these categories of principles, Ackerman and Kruegler (1994) offer a cohesive strategy for participants in nonviolent action. Their work makes clear that while nonviolent action is bottom-up in nature, success ultimately requires strategic planning and adjustment depending on the specific context and changes in that context.

A subsequent book, *A Force More Powerful*, by Ackerman and DuVall (2000) was adapted for a PBS documentary of the same name. The book and documentary popularize the idea of nonviolent struggle as an alternative to violence. For Ackerman and Kruegler (1994) and Ackerman and DuVall (2000), understanding and appreciating nonviolent action is crucial because, in their estimation, it has proven to be the most effective, least costly, method of creating positive social change.

Boulding (1999) offers insight into the different "faces of power" that exist in society. The first type of power is "threat power" which is power based on the threat of force. One example of this are laws backed by state force. The second type of power is "economic power" grounded in the distribution of wealth. Finally, there is "integrative power" which refers to the "power of persuasion, legitimacy, fairness, community, etc." (Boulding 1999, 10–11). Integrative power is the most important because it is the source of the other forms of power. As Boulding (1999, 11) puts it, "threat power and economic power are difficult to exercise if they are not supported by integrative power, that is they are not seen as legitimate." Within Boulding's framework, all three faces of power co-exist but it is integrative power which grants legitimacy or illegitimacy to other types of power. Threat power depends on the threat of force, but also on the response of the person being threatened who can choose to submit or to defy the threatening party. Likewise, economic power is not just the result of seller behavior but also buyer behavior. Like Sharp, Boulding's work highlights that the source of power is ultimately found in the populace and the ordinary people have the choice to consent or refrain from cooperating. This power is the foundation of nonviolent action.

Another strand of literature focuses on the link between globalization, modernization, and nonviolent action. Carter (2005) analyzes nonviolent action (what she calls "direct action") in both repressive regimes and democratic states. She links the rise of nonviolent action to modernizing trends including the centralization of state power and calls for limits on that power, the spread of democratic values and beliefs, industrialization, and new communication technologies. In Carter's framework, nonviolent action is understood both as a response to the lack of democracy, as well as a mechanism for democratic empowerment. Her analysis also focuses on the impact of globalization on nonviolent action. Carter contends that globalization has created both a desire and a means for greater coordination between nation states in direct action. Institutions like the international criminal courts, the United Nations, the World Bank, and various NGOs transcend the boundaries of the nation-state. Technological advances, such as the internet, lower the cost of activists coordinating their efforts across geopolitical boundaries. Carter believes that these trends create special opportunities for direct action on a global scale.

Carter (2012) analyzes key issues with civil resistance in the context of current global struggles. In doing so, she raises a number of important issues for consideration. For example, she notes that the distinction between nonviolent campaigns and violent campaigns is often blurred. She points to the guerrilla warfare in South Africa and the Philippines which occurred simultaneously with civil resistance. She also notes that historical instances of property destruction alongside a nonviolent campaign are common. Carter challenges us to reconsider how we define revolutions in an age where nonviolent action is increasingly commonplace. This requires clarification of what constitutes a revolution, coups d'état, and rebellion. In doing so, she also presents an opportunity to think about how violent and nonviolent action may serve to reinforce one another, or be at odds with one another, in terms of achieving the desired goals.

Research by Sharon Erickson Nepstad focuses on security force responses as a method of nonviolent action. Nepstad (2011) presents a spectrum of military actions including loyalty, shirking, selective compliance, desertion, outright disobedience, defection, and mutiny. In her analysis, any move toward defection is positive for civil resistance movements. Shirking is a method of noncompliance that police or military use that often does not result in punishment for insubordination. Selective compliance occurs when security forces obey certain orders but do not comply with others. For example, a police officer may say that he will enforce traffic laws, but he will not shoot into a crowd of protesters. Desertion occurs when individuals leave without permission. Disobedience is when members of the security force refuse to support the state, but they do not ally with the movement. Mutiny occurs when security forces abandon the state, and then they join the cause of the resistance movement. Understanding how these military actions both represent forms of nonviolent action and might influence broader nonviolent movements for better or worse is an important area of research.

Nepstad (2013) analyzes the state's methods of maintaining loyalty. The state may punish (or threaten to punish) troops who are disloyal. The state may provide troops with economic incentives for maintaining the regime. It may also provide troops with political incentives for maintaining the regime. She also considers tactics for civil resistors to encourage defections including raising the political costs of regime loyalty, raising the moral costs of regime loyalty, raising the honor costs of regime loyalty, and lowering the personal costs of defecting. There are also structural factors that may be relevant. For example, the military's structural design matters for whether and how loyalty is maintained. Moreover, a nation's natural resources and wealth may play a contributing factor in strategies related to nonviolent action, as might a regime's international ties and alliances.

Chenoweth and Stephan (2011) and Chenoweth and Lewis (2013) have created several data sets (the Nonviolent and Violent Campaigns and Outcomes (NAVCO) database) to compare violent methods of defense to nonviolent methods.[2] Chenoweth and Stephan (2011) use this data to analyze whether violent or nonviolent action is more effective in bringing about regime change. Combining empirical analysis with case studies, Chenoweth and Stephan find that nonviolent methods are more successful than violent methods at instituting a new regime. They argue that reduced barriers to entry and alternate forms of human and physical capital induce greater numbers to join a civil resistance movement, as opposed to violent resistance. In contrast to nonviolent action, violence requires certain physical and social capital that often prohibits large portions of the population from participating. In the absence of these constraints, nonviolence allows for greater participation by the populace. They also find that larger populations within civil resistance movements are a key indicator of success. The underlying logic is that a larger number of resistors projects greater power against the target of the civil resistance.

Recent empirical studies have built on Chenoweth and Stephan's original work to advance our understanding of the various aspects of nonviolent action. Sutton et al. (2014) use the NAVCO database to analyze the role of media in nonviolent campaigns. They find that the strength of existing institutions, and particularly the existence of a parallel media, are important for a nonviolent movement's ability to use the tactic of political jiu-jitsu effectively.

Bayer et al. (2016) empirically analyze the effect of nonviolent action on the sustainability of democratic regimes. They find that democratic governments that experience nonviolent action during the transition phase last longer than those that do not. They explain this finding by suggesting that the organizational culture associated with nonviolent action has spillover effects which foster democratic survival through time.

Bethke (2017) employs the NAVOC database to study how nonviolent action affects democratic consolidation. Consolidation refers to a democratic regime that has become stable such that a return to a nondemocratic government is unlikely. In order to operationalize democratic consolidation, Bethke relies on Huntington's (1968) two-turnover test. The first turnover occurs when the party that won the first election (Party A) after the transition losses a subsequent election and peacefully turns over power to the winner (Party B). The second turnover occurs when Party B subsequently loses an election and likewise turns over power peacefully. When two turnovers occur, Huntington contends, it indicates that the democracy is consolidated. Bethke (2017) finds that initiating a democratic transition through nonviolent action is not necessarily beneficial for the first turnover. But given that a first turnover has occurred, nonviolent action increases the likelihood of a successful second turnover. He hypothesizes that the effect of nonviolent action may take time to develop and manifest, such that nonviolent action doesn't have a significant impact on the first turnover but does on the second.

Another strand of scholarship focuses on the extremity of acts of civil disobedience. To analyze this topic, Glaeser and Sunstein (2015) develop a rational-choice model of civil disobedience. In their theory, acts of civil disobedience are about signaling on two margins. One is to signal, to both the political elite and other citizens, that government leaders have engaged in actions which citizens find unsatisfactory. In this scenario acts of civil disobedience may be a sufficient signal to engender change. Second, acts of civil disobedience can be used to provoke political elites to signal their own negative behavior through their response to the protestors. When done correctly, civil disobedience can provoke authorities to publicly reveal their true type. The authors discuss both types of signals and develop a number of empirical propositions regarding civil disobedience.

There is also scholarship at the intersection of nonviolent action and legal studies. Wilson (2016) leverages the research on nonviolent action as the basis for a bottom-up approach to international human rights law. People power, she suggests, may be able to solve many of the issues related to human rights abuses abroad. Her interdisciplinary legal framework encourages nonviolent action, emphasizing the spontaneous development of law through the actions of the citizenry.

When advocating people power, Wilson makes a distinction between front-end and back-end people power. Front-end people power refers to the power of citizens to form a government associated with social contract theory. Using Poland as a case study, she notes the work of civil society to imagine and construct governmental structures through nonviolent action. Back-end people power is relevant in situations where there is a dormant social contract between a government and citizens. In this context, citizens have the power to prevent government abuse through nonviolent action. Wilson advocates the creation of a "privilege of nonviolence" ensuring that government agents should not arrest, torture, or use physical violence against citizens using nonviolent action. She sees this legal principle as a way to empower civil resistance and provide incentives for increased use of nonviolent methods.

Another strand of literature focuses on the interplay between nonviolent action and economic factors. Butcher and Svensson (2014) focus on why civil resistance movements begin. They note that participation in nonviolent action involves a collective action problem at both the individual and intergroup levels where participants must be assured that others will join their group and actively participate. They contend that economically interdependent social networks can be leveraged to overcome these collective action problems. Empirically, they find a correlation between the percent of GDP in manufacturing and civil resistance. They also find that countries without a large manufacturing sector tend toward violent insurrection.

Butcher et al. (2018) argue that the existence of organized labor increases the chance of success in civil resistance movements. The underlying idea is that organized labor can leverage its relationship with the state to effectively interact to obtain credible commitments from government. Organized labor movements are also likely to possess the social networks and capital necessary for effective civil resistance. Empirically, the authors find a correlation between national trade union participation and successful civil resistance.

There is also research exploring the connection between nonviolent action, geography, and regime transitions. Butcher (2017) focuses on the distance from the capital city in instances of both nonviolent and violent action. He finds that civil resistance movements are most likely to achieve regime transitions with large protests inside of the capital city. The underlying idea is that a key aspect of success in nonviolent action is symbolism. In most societies, the capital city serves as a symbol of importance and power relative to the geographic periphery outside of the capital. Nonviolent action that takes place within the capital city is able to leverage this symbolism. Butcher also finds that violent insurrections are more likely to succeed in overthrowing the current regime if the conflict takes place within the capital city.

A final strand of literature focuses on operationalizing the insights from prior research and experience with nonviolent action. Perhaps the best example of this is the work of Srđa Popović, the founder of the Center for Applied Nonviolent Action and Strategies who helped organize Otpor! ("Resistance!" in English), the student movement which was central to the fall of Slobodan Milošević in Serbia. Otpor! applied Gene Sharp's methods in Serbia which included undermining the regime through the use of subversive symbols, underground concerts where political speeches were made, public demonstrations and marches, graffiti, the distribution of leaflets, and various forms of humor about the ruling regime. By employing these methods, the organization created social incentives to join or be arrested for the cause. Based on Otpor!'s success, Milošević officially classified it as a terrorist organization, which only served to strengthen the organization while diminishing the credibility of the regime.

Based on the work of Sharp, as well as his own experiences in Serbia, Popović created a curriculum outlining how to wage a successful nonviolent campaign (Popović et al. 2007). He also documented his tactics and experiences with nonviolent action in *Blueprint for Revolution* (Popović and Miller 2015). Through the Center for Applied Nonviolent Action and Strategies, he has worked in 50 countries, including Iran, Zimbabwe, Burma, Venezuela, Ukraine, Georgia, Palestine, Western Sahara, West Papua, Eritrea, Belarus, Azerbaijan, Tonga, Tunisia, and Egypt.[3]

3.5   Conclusion

Nonviolent action is a crucial form of bottom-up action for citizens to deal with a variety of crisis situations. There are several areas for future research. One involves continuing to document nonviolent action in a variety of contexts and settings. As noted, there is a growing empirical literature that looks at the variables influencing success and failure in nonviolent action. While these studies can offer general insights into the factors that matter for successful nonviolent action, detailed, micro-level case studies are crucial for understanding why nonviolent action was successful in some instances and not others.

These case studies may benefit from drawing on three existing literatures. The first focuses on scholarship identifying a range of "selective incentives" to solve collective action problems (Olson 1965; Tullock 1971; Lichbach 1994, 1995). As noted, some of the existing literature on nonviolent action has begun to focus on the role of incentives in certain aspects of nonviolence, such as the civil rights movement in America (Chong 1991) and the behavior of security forces (Nepstad 2011, 2013). Further exploring the array of incentives facing various parties and groups in specific contexts will offer important insights into why some instances of nonviolence were successful or unsuccessful.

There are a number of important collective action challenges to consider. What factors contribute to the formation of groups engaged in nonviolent action? How does a critical mass agree to work together to respond to a crisis? How does a critical mass coordinate on nonviolence, especially given the potential for a violent response to nonviolence? What factors contribute to, or undermine, group cohesion over time? Under what conditions do groups persist until the end goal is achieved, and under what conditions does the group unravel prior to achieving its goals?

Another relevant literature considers how people coordinate in non-price environments and the role that social entrepreneurship plays in the coordinating process (Chamlee-Wright and Myers 2008; Chamlee-Wright 2010; Chamlee-Wright and Storr 2009, 2010a, b, 2011a, b, 2014; Storr, Grube, et al. 2017; Storr, Haeffele-Balch, et al. 2015, 2017).

To date, much of the scholarship in this area has focused on recovery in the wake of natural disasters, but these same insights are relevant for understanding success or failure in nonviolent action which also takes place in nonpriced environments. Extending this literature to nonviolent action will offer insight into the role that social entrepreneurs play in discovering opportunities for nonviolent action and for understanding the processes of coordination associated with nonviolent action.

A third literature focuses on the dynamics of spontaneous, or emergent, orders (Hayek 2014). Scholarship in this area identifies several key features of emergent orders. First, they are the result of purposeful human action, but not human design. Second, they can meaningfully be described as orders meaning there are clear, identifiable patterns which are the result of interrelated elements. Third, there are feedback mechanisms (both positive and negative) which guide the behavior of actors in the system. Fourth, actors in the system follow rules of conduct (both formal and informal) which guide their behavior and influence the type of order that emerges. Sixth, they are abstract meaning that since the order is not the result of human design, participants do not need to fully understand the nuances of the overall order. One line of future research is to explore nonviolent action as an example of spontaneous order. A related line of research is to analyze individual cases of nonviolent action in light of the defining features of spontaneous orders outlined above. This would shed light on the nuances of nonviolent action across a variety of contexts.

There are four other areas of study where research on nonviolent action is relevant. The first is scholarship on state building and nation building. Nonviolent action offers a potential indigenous mechanism for institutional change that relies on local actors. This reliance on indigenous sources of change may lead to institutional changes which are more sustainable and "sticky" over time (Boettke et al. 2008). As an indigenous mechanism of institutional change, nonviolence stands in contrast to exogenous forms of institutional change such as external aid and military force which are often viewed as necessary to displace existing institutions. Understanding where and when nonviolence is feasible as a means of successful institutional change has important implications for those working in international relations and development economics.

Second, further work is needed to explore the relationship between violent and nonviolent action. As discussed in the Introduction, nonviolent and violent actions are conceptually distinct. But, in practice, this distinction is not always clear. For example, Cobb (2014) considers the relationship between violence and nonviolence in the African American civil rights movement in America in the 1950s and 1960s. He argues that while nonviolence did play a key role in the movement, so too did self-defense through the threat of violence by those engaged in nonviolent action. Armed defenders often provided crucial protection to the organizations involved in nonviolent actions. This raises a number of important and open questions that are relevant to all nonviolent action. What is the relationship between violent and nonviolent action? To what extent are these two categories complements, and to what extent are they substitutes? Under what conditions does violent action reinforce the goals of nonviolent action, and under what conditions does it undermine those goals? Answering these questions is important for understanding the distinctions between violent and nonviolent action and how they relate in practice.

Third, there is research to be done on how nonviolent action can empower the weakest members of society in their daily lives. Much of the focus of scholarship on nonviolent action focuses on nonviolent action in the context of groups and movements. While this is certainly important, nonviolent action can be employed by individuals in a variety of settings. For example, Scott (1985) shows how nonviolent action is used by ordinary individuals as a weapon against domination. As he notes, "Most of the political life of subordinate groups is to be found neither in the overt collective defiance of powerholders, nor in complete hegemonic compliance, but in the vast territory between these two polar opposites" (Scott 1985, 136). This is important because it highlights that nonviolent action is not limited solely to organized groups or to one-off visible historical events. In doing so, it demonstrates the widespread relevance of nonviolent action for understanding the world.

Finally, the research on nonviolence offers a radical alternative to the widely accepted view that security and defense must be provided by the state. The view that the state must be the sole provider of defense is well established in economics and political science (Coyne 2015). As Sharp (1985, 1990b, 1992, 2001) makes clear, however, individual citizens possess the power to defend against both internal and external threats. Exploring the various aspects of citizen-based, polycentric defense remains an open area for future research. This research will benefit by drawing on the aforementioned literatures and insights to understand the ability of individuals to provide effective security and defense. In doing so, it will contribute to our understanding of nonviolent action as a crucial bottom-up response to crises.

Notes

1. The literature on nonviolent action is silent regarding the normative content of the goals of the nonviolent efforts. In principle, nonviolent action could be used for beneficial outcomes—for example, protecting or expanding human rights and civil liberties—or to harm certain people or groups—for example, undermining rights and liberties.
2. According to the NAVCO Data Project website (NAVCO n.d.): "The Nonviolent and Violent Campaigns and Outcomes (NAVCO) Data Project is a multi-level data collection effort that catalogues major nonviolent and violent resistance campaigns around the globe from 1900 to 2013. The project produces aggregate-level data on resistance campaigns from 1900 to 2013 (NAVCO 1), annual data on campaign behavior from 1946 to 2013 (NAVCO 2), and events data on tactical selection in a sample of 26 countries with major nonviolent and violent campaigns from 1991 to 2012 (NAVCO 3)."
3. For information on the center, see https://canvasopedia.org/about-us/.

References

Ackerman, P., and C. Kruegler. 1994. *Strategic Nonviolent Conflict: The Dynamics of People Power in the Twentieth Century*. Westport, CT: Praeger.
Ackerman, P., and J. DuVall. 2000. *A Force More Powerful: A Century of Nonviolent Conflict*. New York: Palgrave Macmillan.

Alinsky, S. 1989. *Rules for Radicals: A Practical Primer for Realistic Radicals*. New York: Vintage Books.

Ammons, J., and C.J. Coyne. 2018. Gene Sharp: The 'Clausewitz of Nonviolent Warfare'. *The Independent Review* 23 (1): 149–156.

Bayer, M., F.S. Bethke, and D. Lambach. 2016. The Democratic Dividend of Nonviolent Resistance. *Journal of Peace Research* 53 (6): 758–771.

Bedau, H.A., ed. 1969. *Civil Disobedience: Theory and Practice*. New York: Pegasus.

Bethke, F.S. 2017. Nonviolent Resistance and Peaceful Turnover of Power. *Peace Economics, Peace Science and Public Policy* 23 (4): 1–5.

Bhattacharya, B. 1977. *Mahatma Gandhi*. New Delhi: Arnold Heinemann Publishers.

Bleiker, R. 1993. *Nonviolent Struggle and the Revolution in East Germany*. Boston: Albert Einstein Institution.

Boettke, P.J., C.J. Coyne, and P.T. Leeson. 2008. Institutional Stickiness and the New Development Economics. *The American Journal of Economics and Sociology* 67 (2008): 331–358.

Boulding, K.E. 1999. Non-Violence and Power in the Twentieth Century. In *Nonviolent Social Movements: A Geographical Perspective*, ed. S. Zunes, L.R. Kurtz, and S.B. Asher, 9–17. Oxford: Blackwell.

Brock, P. 1968. *Radical Pacifists in Antebellum America*. Princeton: Princeton University Press.

Butcher, C. 2017. Geography and the Outcomes of Civil Resistance and Civil War. *Third World Quarterly* 38 (7): 1454–1472.

Butcher, C., J.L. Gray, and L. Mitchell. 2018. Striking It Free? Organized Labor and the Success of Civil Resistance. *Journal of Global Security Studies* 3 (3): 302–321.

Butcher, C., and I. Svensson. 2014. Manufacturing Dissent: Modernization and the Onset of Major Nonviolent Resistance Campaigns. *Journal of Conflict Resolution* 60 (2): 311–339.

Carter, A. 1995. *Mahatma Gandhi: A Selected Bibliography*. Wesport, CT: Greenwood Press.

———. 2005. *Direct Action and Democracy Today*. Malden, MA: Polity Press.

———. 2012. *People Power and Political Change: Key Issues and Concepts*. New York: Routledge.

Chamlee-Wright, E. 2010. *The Cultural and Political Economy of Recovery: Social Learning in a Post-Disaster Environment*. New York: Routledge.

Chamlee-Wright, E., and J. Myers. 2008. Discovery and Social Learning in Non-Priced Environments: An Austrian View of Social Network Theory. *The Review of Austrian Economics* 21 (2/3): 151–166.

Chamlee-Wright, E., and V.H. Storr. 2009. Club Goods and Post-Disaster Community Return. *Rationality & Society* 21 (4): 429–458.

———. 2010a. The Role of Social Entrepreneurship in Post-Katrina Community Recovery. *International Journal of Innovation and Regional Development* 2 (1/2): 149–164.

———. 2010b. Expectations of Government Response to Disaster. *Public Choice* 144 (1–2): 253–274.

———. 2011a. Social Capital, Lobbying and Community-Based Interest Groups. *Public Choice* 149 (1–2): 167–185.

———. 2011b. Social Capital as Collective Narratives and Post-Disaster Community Recovery. *The Sociological Review* 59 (2): 266–282.

———. 2014. Commercial Relationships and Spaces After Disaster. *Society* 51 (6): 656–664.

Chenoweth, E., and O.A. Lewis. 2013. Unpacking Nonviolent Campaigns: Introducing the NAVCO 2.0 Dataset. *Journal of Peace Research* 50 (3): 415–423.

Chenoweth, E., and M.J. Stephan. 2011. *Why Civil Resistance Works: The Strategic Logic of Nonviolent Conflict*. New York: Columbia University Press.

Chodorov, F. 1980. *Fugitive Essays: Selected Writings of Frank Chodorov*. Indianapolis: Liberty Press.

Chomsky, N. 1969. *American Power and the New Mandarins*. New York: Pantheon Books.

Chong, D. 1991. *Collection Action and the Civil Rights Movement*. Chicago: University of Chicago Press.

Cobb, C.E., Jr. 2014. *This Nonviolent Stuff'll Get You Killed: How Guns Made the Civil Rights Movement Possible*. New York: Basic Books.

Coyne, C.J. 2015. Lobotomozing the Defense Brain. *The Review of Austrian Economics* 28 (4): 371–396.

Crosby, E.H. 1905. *Garrison, the Non-Resistant*. Chicago: The Public Publishing Company.

Dillon, M.L. 1974. *The Abolitionists: The Growth of a Dissenting Minority*. DeKalb: Northern Illinois University Press.

Gandhi, M.K. 1993. *An Autobiography: The Story of My Experiments with Truth*. Boston: Beacon Press.

Glaeser, E.L., and C. Sunstein. 2015. *A Theory of Civil Disobedience*. NBER Working Paper No. 21338. http://www.nber.org/papers/w21338.

Gramsci, A. 2011. *Letters from Prison*. Edited by F. Rosengarten and Translated by R. Rosenthal. New York: Columbia University Press.

Hayek, F.A. 2014. *The Collected Works of F.A. Hayek*. In *Volume 15: The Market and Other Orders*, ed. B. Caldwell. Chicago: University of Chicago Press.

Hirschman, A.O. Exit. 1970. *Voice, and Loyalty*. Cambridge: Harvard University Press.

Hunt, J.D. 1986. *Gandhi and the Nonconformists: Encounters in South Africa*. New Delhi: Promilla & Company Publishers.

Huntington, S.P. 1968. *Political Order in Changing Societies*. New Haven: Yale University Press.

King, M.L., Jr. 1981. *Strength to Love*. Philadelphia: Fortress Press.

———. 2010. *Stride Toward Freedom: The Montgomery Story*. Boston: Beacon Press.

Kraditor, A. 1989. *Means and Ends in American Abolitionism: Garrison and His Critics on Strategy and Tactics, 1834–1850*. Chicago: Ivan R. Dee.

La Boétie, E. [1735] 1942. *The Discourse of Voluntary Servitude*. Translated by H. Kurz. Indianapolis: Liberty Fund.

Lichbach, M.I. 1994. Rethinking Rationality and Rebellion: Theories of Collective Action and Problems of Collective Dissent. *Rationality and Society* 6 (1): 8–39.

———. 1995. *The Rebel's Dilemma: Collective Action and Collective Dissent*. Ann Arbor: University of Michigan Press.

Manning, C.A. 1943. Thoreau and Tolstoy. *The New England Quarterly* 16 (2): 234–243.

Mattaini, M.A. 2013. *Strategic Nonviolent Power: The Science of Satyagraha*. Edmonton: AU Press.

Nāga, K. 1950. *Tolstoy and Gandhi, No. 4*. Patna: Pustak Bhandar.

Nepstad, S.E. 2011. *Nonviolent Revolutions: Civil Resistance in the Late 20th Century*. New York: Oxford University Press.

———. 2013. Mutiny and Nonviolence in the Arab Spring: Exploring Military Defections and Loyalty in Egypt, Bahrain, and Syria. *Journal of Peace Research* 50 (3): 337–349.

NAVCO. n.d. *NAVCO Data Project*. Sié Chéou-Kang Center for International Security & Diplomacy, University of Denver. https://www.du.edu/korbel/sie/research/chenow_navco_data.html.

Oates, S.B. 1994. *Let the Trumpet Sound: A Life of Martin Luther King, Jr.* New York: Harper Perennial.

Olson, M. 1965. *The Logic of Collective Action.* Cambrige: Harvard University Press.

Piven, F.F., and R.A. Cloward. 1979. *Poor People's Movements: Why They Succeed, How They Fail.* New York: Vintage Books.

Popović, S., and M. Miller. 2015. *Blueprint for Revolution: How to Use Rice Pudding, Lego Men, and Other Nonviolent Techniques to Galvanize Communities, Overthrow Dictators, or Simply Change the World.* New York: Spiegel & Grau.

Popović, S., S. Djinovic, A. Milivojevic, H. Merriman, and I. Marovic. 2007. *A Guide to Effective Nonviolent Struggle: Students Book.* Belgrade: Centre for Applied NonViolent Action and Strategies, CANVAS Core Curriculum.

Powers, R.S., W.B. Vogele, C. Kruegler, and R.M. McCarthy. 2011. *Protest, Power, and Change: An Encyclopedia of Nonviolent Action from ACT-UP to Women's Suffrage.* New York: Routledge.

Proudfoot, M. 1962. *Diary of a Sit-in.* Chapel Hill, NC: University of North Carolina Press.

Rediker, M. 2017. *The Fearless Benjamin Lay: The Quaker Dwarf Who Became the First Revolutionary Abolitionist.* Boston: Beacon Press.

Roberts, S. 2018. Gene Sharp, Global Guru of Nonviolence Resistance, Dies at 90. *The New York Times*, February 2. https://www.nytimes.com/2018/02/02/obituaries/gene-sharp-global-guru-of-nonviolent-resistance-dies-at-90.html.

Robinson, J.A. 1981. *Abraham Went Out: A Biography of A.J. Muste.* Philadelphia: Temple University Press.

Scott, J.C. 1985. *Weapons of the Weak: Everyday Forms of Peasant Resistance.* New Haven, CT: Yale Universsity Press.

Sharp, G. 1960. *Gandhi Wields the Weapon of Moral Power: Three Case Histories.* Ahmedabad: Navajivan Publishing House.

———. 1961. *Gandhi Faces the Storm.* Ahmedabad: Navajivan Publishing House.

———. 1970a. *Exploring Nonviolent Alternatives.* Boston: Extending Horizons Books.

———. 1970b. *National Security Through Civilian Based Defense.* Omaha: Association for Transarmament Studies.

———. 1973. *The Politics of Nonviolent Action, 3 Parts.* Boston: Porter Sargent.

———. 1979. *Gandhi as a Political Strategist.* Boston: Porter Sargent.

———. 1980a. *Social Power and Political Freedom.* Boston: Extending Horizons Books.

———. 1980b. *Making the Abolition of War a Realistic Goal*. Boston: The Albert Einstein Institution.

———. 1985. *Making Europe Unconquerable: The Potential of Civilian Based Deterrence and Defense*. Cambridge: Ballinger.

———. 1990a. *The Role of Power in Nonviolent Struggle, Monograph Series*. Vol. 3. Boston: The Albert Einstein Institution.

———. 1990b. *Civilian-Based Defense: A Post-Military Weapons System*. Princeton: Princeton University Press.

———. 1992. *Self-Reliant Defense Without Bankruptcy or War*. Boston: The Albert Einstein Institution.

———. 1994. *From Dictatorship to Democracy: A Conceptual Framework for Liberation*. Boston: The Albert Einstein Institution.

———. 2001. *The Anti-Coup*. Boston: The Albert Einstein Institution.

———. 2005. *Waging Nonviolent Struggle: 20th Century Practice and 21st Century Potential*. Boston: Porter Sargent.

———. 2010a. *There Are Realistic Alternatives*. Boston: The Albert Einstein Institution.

———. 2010b. *Self-Liberation: A Guide to Strategic Planning to End a Dictatorship or Other Oppression*. Boston: The Albert Einstein Institution.

———. 2013. *How Nonviolent Struggle Works*. Boston: The Albert Einstein Institution.

Storr, V.H., L.E. Grube, and S. Haeffele-Balch. 2017. Polycentric Orders and Post-Disaster Recovery: A Case Study of One Orthodox Jewish Community Following Hurricane Sandy. *Journal of Institutional Economics* 13 (4): 875–897.

Storr, V.H., S. Haeffele-Balch, and L.E. Grube. 2015. *Community Revival in the Wake of Disaster: Lessons in Local Entrepreneurship*. New York: Palgrave Macmillan.

———. 2017. Social Capital and Social Learning After Hurricane Sandy. *The Review of Austrian Economics* 30 (4): 447–467.

Sutton, J., C. Butcher, and I. Svensson. 2014. Explaining Political Jiu-Jitsu: Institution-Building and the Outcomes of Regime Violence Against Unarmed Protests. *Journal of Peace Research* 51 (5): 559–573.

Thoreau, H.D. 1963. *On the Duty of Civil Disobedience*. London: Peace News Ltd.

———. 1969. *A Yankee in Canada: With Anti-Slavery and Reform Papers*. Boston: Ticknor and Fields.

Tolstoy, L. 1885. *What I Believe*. London: Elliot Stock.

———. 2012. *The Kingdom of God Is Within You*. New York: Simon & Schuster.

Tullock, G. 1971. The Paradox of Revolution. *Public Choice* 11 (1): 89–99.

Wilson, E.A. 2016. People Power and the Problem of Sovereignty in International Law. *Duke Journal of Comparative & International Law* 26 (551): 551–594.

Wink, W. 2000. *Peace Is the Way: Writings on Nonviolence from the Fellowship of Reconciliation*. Ossining, NY: Orbis Books.

4

The Private Sector's Contribution to Natural Disaster Response

Steven Horwitz

4.1 Introduction

Of all of the issues that generate debate over the size and role of government relative to the private sector, natural disaster relief tends to be one where almost everyone assumes that government, especially at the national level, should have a very large role. Even raising the question of expecting the private sector to play a large and positive role in disaster relief will cause responses from skepticism to incredulity. However plausible those responses might seem to be on the surface, the history of natural disaster relief tells a very different story. In particular, the private sector played a central and irreplaceable role in more recent disaster responses, especially during and after Hurricane Katrina. In this chapter, I review both the recent history of these private sector responses and offer a series of explanations for the private sector's general effectiveness in comparison to government-driven response and relief programs. This analysis does

S. Horwitz (✉)
Department of Economics, Ball State University, Muncie, IN, USA
e-mail: sghorwitz@bsu.edu

© The Author(s) 2020   **57**
S. Haeffele, V. H. Storr (eds.), *Bottom-up Responses to Crisis*, Mercatus Studies
in Political and Social Economy, https://doi.org/10.1007/978-3-030-39312-0_4

not necessarily deny that there are things that government can do that others cannot, but it does suggest that a more thorough understanding of what the private sector is able to do is crucial for knowing who is better positioned to engage in the necessary response and recovery efforts.

4.2   What Has the Private Sector Done?

Although the focus of this chapter will be on the response to Hurricane Katrina and other storms since, the private sector and civil society have played a long-standing role in responding to various sorts of disasters. In the famous and disastrous Chicago Fire of 1871, the relief effort was largely directed by the Chicago Relief and Aid Society, with government's role mostly restricted to maintaining law and order (Skarbek 2014). Most observers at the time applauded the work of the Society in getting help to those who needed it, which included getting small businesses back on their feet. The private sector response to the San Francisco earthquake of 1906 was perhaps even more impressive (Coate 2011; Edwards 2017). Insurance companies covered almost all of their claims, and firms in industries from banking to railroads acted to both get running again and to help directly with relief. For example, the Southern Pacific Railroad offered free evacuation to over 200,000 residents. In the Great Easter Flood of 1913, several midwestern states were heavily damaged. In hard-hit Dayton, Ohio, the National Cash Register Company coordinated the entire relief project, from building boats to providing food and shelter for the city's displaced residents. They also opened their headquarters to the Red Cross and National Guard (Edwards 2017). Before the dramatic increase in government responsibility for natural and economic disasters that was part of the New Deal, the private and charitable sectors played a significant and effective role in disaster response.

Even as the visible activities of government agencies, and their desire to take credit for whatever successes took place, have dominated the relief process, since then the private sector has still played an important role. This was especially clear in the response to Hurricane Katrina along the Gulf Coast in 2005.[1] After Katrina struck New Orleans and other parts of the Gulf Coast, both governments and the private sector moved into action. The response of the Federal Emergency Management Agency (FEMA) was both late and ineffective, with the agency the subject of much-deserved criticism. In some places, it was as long as ten full days until FEMA arrived and began to do much of anything. In the meantime, local and national businesses responded to the crisis by moving goods into the stricken region and working to get stores open and stocked as quickly as possible. In some cases, they gave away goods to local residents and provided necessities such as medicines for those in need.

Of those private sector actors, Walmart was the biggest and most effective. Between the landfall of Katrina on August 29th and September 16th, Walmart brought almost 2500 truckloads of goods into the areas hit by the hurricane. Once those supplies arrived, they also had drivers and trucks at the ready to get those necessities to a variety of organizations in the communities affected by the storm. In addition to Walmart, Home Depot played an active role in the relief effort, providing over 800 truckloads of its own in addition to providing transportation for 1000 of its own employees into the Gulf Coast area to help with the distribution process. Walmart and other private sector firms gave a good deal of this merchandise away to local residents of the most devastated areas. In addition to the areas directly affected, Walmart sent several truckloads of goods to Houston where Gulf Coast evacuees found temporary quarters at the Astrodome and the Brown Convention Center. Firms like Walmart and Home Depot were able to get these supplies to all of these areas within hours of the storm having passed. This response was much more timely than that of FEMA and other government agencies, which often took days, if not weeks, to provide any meaningful relief.

In addition to giving away needed supplies, private sector firms did an exceptional job at getting stores damaged by the storm re-opened quickly. Walmart had 126 stores and two distribution centers closed at the height of the storm, more than half of which lost power and 89 of which had some kind of damage, including some that were flooded. However, only ten days after landfall, all but 15 of the stores and both of the distribution centers had re-opened, with only those stores that had severe flooding or structural damage remaining closed. McDonald's also was able to re-open stores quickly. At one point, over 500 of their restaurants were closed by either power outages or damage, but 80 percent of those stores were open within a week of Katrina's landfall. Proctor & Gamble's sponsorship of their Tide Detergent's "Loads of Hope" program is worth noting here as well. After Katrina, they used trucks and vans to create mobile laundromats that could go to disaster areas and provide free washing and drying services for residents who are unable to use their own machines or local laundromats. This program continues today but was created as part of their response to Katrina. Loads of Hope has provided help to over 45,000 victims of natural disasters since its implementation.[2]

Since Katrina, the private sector has continued to play a crucial role in the immediate response and recovery processes after several natural disasters. Local residents praised the role of local and national businesses in the recovery from the devastating tornadoes in Joplin, Missouri in 2011 (Smith and Sutter 2013). Walmart has been involved in relief efforts in a variety of fairly localized flooding events across the US. In May of 2016, the Canadian province of Alberta was hit by a huge forest fire that severely damaged the town of Fort McMurray and caused more than 60,000 people to abandon their homes. That area is oil country and several energy companies responded by trucking in food, providing free oil and gasoline, and donating various kinds of vehicles to transport evacuees away from the fire (Horwitz 2016). And even more recently, a large number of private sector firms were instrumental in the response to Hurricane Harvey in Texas and Louisiana in the summer of 2017. Walmart was there again, providing over 2000 truckloads of supplies. HEB Grocery sent mobile kitchens to the Houston area, and those included not just meals but also pharmacy services and ATMs. Anheuser-Busch InBev, as they frequently do during disasters, sent more than 155,000 cans of drinking water (Perry 2017).

During the response to Katrina, the work done by Walmart did not go unnoticed by local government officials. In suburban New Orleans, the president and sheriff of Jefferson Parish praised Walmart for all that they did to get supplies into their areas. The parish president observed that Walmart was able to do all of this despite having their trucks turned back by FEMA on several occasions. The sheriff explicitly compared the superiority of Walmart's response to that of the federal government, noting that if the latter had responded like Walmart that their parish would not have been in a state of crisis. The mayor of another New Orleans suburb credited Walmart with preventing looting by showing up quickly with food and water. Other Gulf Coast communities had similar experiences (Horwitz 2009). Since Katrina, this sort of effective response from the private sector has been the norm and the willingness of local officials and the media to acknowledge it has grown as well.

4.3   Why the Private Sector Is So Effective

From a policy perspective, it is important to understand why the private sector has been so effective at disaster relief. Having a better sense of the reasons for that success can help policymakers in two ways. First, it can provide a set of criteria for judging the appropriateness of giving the private sector maximum leeway. If we know *why* the private sector is so effective, we can determine which sorts of situations are ones in which those reasons will be particularly salient. Second, understanding the sources of private sector success can help us determine what sorts of government responses might be more effective by seeing whether those agencies work in ways that capture at least some of the benefits that are associated with the private sector.

The foundation of the market economy is that in order to make profits, firms must provide the goods and services that consumers demand, and do so at prices at which they are willing to purchase them. In competitive markets, firms that are unable to get that job done will find themselves making losses and will be forced to either change their ways or cease operations. Successful firms are able to both correctly anticipate what people want and adjust well when their anticipations are incorrect. Profitable firms also must make good decisions about how they produce their outputs, as profitability requires both responsiveness to consumer demand and attention to cost so that the process of producing those outputs actually adds value.

Crucial to the ability of private sector firms to do all of these things is the price system. As has long been recognized in economics, market prices serve as knowledge surrogates that guide the decision making of market actors (Hayek 1945). Prices inform firms as they formulate their production plans and the budgets associated with them, helping them sort out which outputs, and what combination of inputs, appear to create the most value for consumers. Prices also tell producers after the fact, in the form of profit and losses, how accurate those plans were. Profits indicate value creation while losses indicate the destruction of value. Prices, profits, and losses are reflections of the whole variety of human knowledge and preferences in play in the market. That knowledge is dispersed among billions of people, and it is often contextualized and inarticulate, making it impossible to convey through language or statistics. Instead, through our decisions to buy or sell (or not to do so), we influence prices, which serve as a stand-in for the knowledge that underlies those decisions. We are able to communicate in ways that transcend the limits of language or statistical data.

One of the ways markets enable us to do this is through what F. A. Hayek (1989) called "several property" or the dispersal of property across multiple owners. It's not just that property is "private" but that it is dispersed. This is important because it allows those who possess the already dispersed knowledge to be able to act on that knowledge with property of their own. Given the dispersal of knowledge, we want to have "several property" in order to ensure that those with the best knowledge have the resources to make good decisions. In other words, markets are effective because the ability to make decisions is parceled out across society, which helps to ensure, along with competition, that those with the best local knowledge are able to act most effectively. Markets are, in this way, very much local and bottom-up institutions.

The emphasis on decentralization and bottom-up responses can be misleading when we talk about the private sector and market processes. The success of markets at leading private sector firms to be better than governments at both disaster preparation and response is not just a matter of the decentralized and dispersed nature of property ownership and administrative control, though those are important. All other things equal, decentralized control over resources tends to be better able to mobilize local knowledge and respond to crises with more agility. However, the problem that all decentralized or bottom-up systems must solve is how to *coordinate* those decentralized decision makers in such a way as to ensure outcomes that best meet people's needs. Because so much knowledge is relevant to the effective use of resources—whether during normal times or crises—local, decentralized control over resources is crucial, whether through a bureaucratic structure or several property. But effective resource use also requires some way for those dispersed controllers of resources to make their local knowledge usable by other resource controllers.

This is the role played by the price system in the private sector. Prices make it possible for firms to share their knowledge with each other through their decisions to buy and sell. Prices and profits are a form of social communication that allows decentralized owners of property to learn from each other and thereby better coordinate their activities. Prices and profits guide firms to know how to be prepared, what to make available, and where those resources are needed, and to gain the experience and have the incentive to get it done well. As policy makers consider reforms to improve disaster response, many emphasize the importance of decentralizing the governmental response, often pointing to the success of the private sector or more decentralized government agencies like the Coast Guard. This is good as far as it goes, but decentralization without a coordination process will only achieve so much. In specifying what sort of decentralized political response might be considered, policy makers should also be asked to show how that dispersed decision making power will be coordinated across decision makers. The advantage of the private sector over even decentralized government agencies is that market prices and profit signals provide a way of coordinating the decentralized decision making of the owners of private property.

4.4 Bottom-Up Responses Within Firms

In the context of natural disaster response, the ways in which successful firms have to be nimble and responsive are especially important. Firms like Walmart face the challenge of getting resources to where they are needed every single day. They develop all kinds of internal procedures for assuming that they can get the necessary inventory to the stores that need them as quickly as possible. In Walmart's case, their inventory management processes, including some of the first uses of radio frequency ID tags, were key in fueling their massive success in the 1990s.

Walmart was not the only firm who responded this well. McDonald's offers another example. A franchise operation like McDonald's has a larger challenge in organizing a corporate response than does a more integrated firm like Walmart. Nonetheless, McDonald's laid out a model for disaster response through its corporate-owned stores and then worked with its franchisee-owners as closely as possible to try to ensure that they were abiding by that corporate model. Like Walmart, McDonald's was aware of the impending storm and had trucks prepared to leave its distribution centers to provide supplies just after the storm passed. Part of their ability to re-open most of their stores so quickly was due to that level of preparation (Horwitz 2010).

It should not surprise us that in the face of a natural disaster, firms like Walmart are very good at quickly moving relief supplies to where they are needed. In some sense, they are tested every day in the ways in which responses to natural disasters demand. One additional reason Walmart's response was so effective was that they have their own emergency response center, complete with a weather forecasting team, which exists for exactly these sorts of situations. This enabled them, along with several other firms, to stage resources on the edge of the predicted storm damage so that they could be easily and quickly moved in after the storm passed. Finally, Walmart made sure that this effort was coordinated on the ground by having two vice presidents in New Orleans, complete with satellite phone systems, immediately after the storm ended. Beyond its ability to help firms know what people want, the profit and loss system provides a key incentive for actors in the private sector to take risks and get resources where they need to be.

Because firms in competitive markets get powerful feedback about the effectiveness of their courses of action, they can empower their employees to exercise their responsibilities with a large degree of discretion. If those employees fail, the firm will know about it. During the response to Katrina, this feature of the private sector was a particularly powerful and relevant one. Despite its reputation of being a heavy-handed, top-down organization, one of the interesting features of Walmart and its response to Katrina is the degree to which it trusts its district and store managers to exercise appropriate discretion, and not just during crises. Walmart's structure provides those managers with both the authority and the data to make decisions based on local circumstances and the needs of their specific customers. The then CEO Lee Scott made this clear in a meeting with this senior staff as the storm was advancing on the Gulf Coast: "A lot of you are going to have to make decisions above your level. Make the best decision that you can with the information that's available to you at the time, and, above all, do the right thing" (Rosengrant 2007, 5).

In several cases, store managers did not ask for preapproval from above before allowing both emergency personnel and local residents to take store supplies to meet the urgent needs of the community. Other employees and managers did things like knocking down a warehouse door with a forklift to get at a supply of water for a nearby retirement home, allowing local police who had lost their homes to use a store as a headquarters and make-shift hotel, and running a bulldozer through the store to collect up undamaged basic goods to be piled in the parking lot for community use. The employee with the bulldozer, who was an assistant manager in the Waveland, Mississippi store, also broke into the store's pharmacy to get a supply of drugs to transport to the local hospital. These examples demonstrate the importance of local knowledge and the necessity of giving actors on the spot the ability to use that knowledge as need be. It is also noteworthy that not only did Walmart's management not punish these acts, they praised and encouraged them, despite the ways in which they appear to run counter to the belief that the private sector is motivated by a narrow sense of profit-maximization.[3] In addition to the bottom-up, decentralized response *across* the private sector, private sector firms are better able to take advantage of dispersed control over decision making *within* organizations than is the public sector.

Two other nongovernmental, bottom-up responses to natural disasters should also be considered in this light, even though neither one is truly part of the "private sector." First, the so-called Cajun Navy has played an enormously helpful role in rescuing people from flooding over the last decade or so. It first came to prominence during Hurricane Katrina, where hundreds of local boat owners assisted the Coast Guard and other agencies in rescuing people from rooftops and other flooded areas. Since Katrina, these boat owners have responded to a variety of flooding crises, including Hurricane Harvey in 2017 and Hurricane Florence in 2018. The Cajun Navy is a loose, decentralized organization of people with the equipment and experience to respond to these crises.[4] They also have a simple coordination system, which is using various forms of communication, especially electronic communication and social media, to know where and how intense of a response is needed. This volunteer, civil society organization is a good example of how bottom-up responses outside of the political process can be very effective in disaster relief.

The second bottom-up, decentralized disaster response from outside of government is households themselves.[5] Households play a crucial role in crisis response, serving as shock absorbers as crises affect other institutions. In particular, households are capable of expanding both the number of people they involve and the range of things that they can do in order to engage in disaster response when economic and political institutions are weakened or have failed. In normal times, households provide various goods and services, such as cooked meals or child care. Some households grow their own food as well. In the aftermath of a natural disaster, households both grow in size by combining with other family members or even neighbors to provide shelter, and expand the goods and services they provide, including engaging in home repair, additional food preparation, and providing aid and comfort to friends and family. Over the last century or so, households have greatly narrowed how much of this sort of production that they do, as more people are able to purchase those things on the market. However, disasters change the relative costs of using the market versus doing in things within the household, leading people to do more of the latter. People who live in disaster-prone areas are likely to be more prepared to take on these tasks than are others, enabling households to play this role as a shock absorber during crises. These responses by households are bottom-up and decentralized, but they are so small scale as to not need much of a coordination process. Simple communication processes among family members can often suffice. In considering effective bottom-up responses to disasters, we should not forget volunteer organizations and households as well.

4.5   Rebuilding Community Through the Market[6]

In addition to the narrowly economic effects brought on by the private sector's direct relief efforts, the reopening of commercial enterprises was a big factor in rebuilding a broader sense of community in the areas damaged by Hurricane Katrina. We have seen similar processes at work in disasters since then. For example, many local residents reported great relief at the return to normalcy reflected in the re-opening of a neighborhood McDonald's. The company also provided free food to first responders. They also set up mobile centers in the worst-hit areas where they were cooking basics for police, firemen, EMTs, and other community responders.

Though donating time and material goods helps rebuild community, one underappreciated but key aspect of the private sector's importance is the role played by the physical sites of market interactions. Those spaces are also sites where people cross paths in various ways and for a wide variety of purposes. Despite the claim that it is in the *polity* where we do things together, we spend far more of our regular daily routine in the world of the *agora*, engaged in various forms of exchange. Virgil Henry Storr (2008, 143) says the following about those market spaces:

> A complete concept of the market, in my view, requires that we appreciate that the market is a social space where both economic and extraeconomic relationships are developed and sustained. Markets are not only embedded in the community but can also promote and sustain the community.

Storr's argument is even more powerful when we think about smaller towns or larger cities with clearly defined neighborhoods. In those places, crossing paths with friends or co-workers at the grocery store or the bank or the gas station is not at all unusual.

In the months after Katrina, survivors of the storm along the Gulf Coast consistently reported that one of the most important indicators of recovery was the re-opening of local stores. Beyond being an indicator, those re-opened stores created spaces for residents to re-establish their relationships with other community members, particularly given the ways in which the storm had destroyed both physical and social capital. The social networks that people relied on for local information were disrupted as various forms of electronic communication were not available following the storm. Finding opportunities to interact with neighbors and others in their various social circles were few and far between and largely limited to face-to-face interactions that happened mostly by chance.

The gradual return of the private sector provided an increasing number of opportunities for just this sort of interaction:

> Interviews with residents who returned to the devastated areas of the Gulf Coast reveal a common theme of finding trips to the store, particularly "general store" types of places such as Walgreen's or Wal-Mart, to be not only important economically, but socially, as it provided them with opportunities to reconnect with friends and extended family and to catch up on the latest news in the community. (Horwitz 2010, 186–187)

These sorts of "general stores" were particularly important because they maximized the opportunities for interaction by having both a large variety of goods (increasing the number of different people who would patronize them) and a large number of necessities (increasing the number of trips people were likely to make to a given store). The combination made the general stores a central site for social interaction with neighbors, creating the opportunity to share important information and generally rebuild important social capital. This point is supported by interviews with residents along the damaged areas of the Gulf after Katrina as well as evacuees in Houston. Everything from stores like Walmart or Walgreens to the re-opening of neighborhood restaurants were listed as key events in the reconstruction of their communities because of the opportunities they presented to cross paths with neighbors and friends. The evacuees reported specifically that trips to Walmart often ended up in meeting new people and making new friendships in their new home. Giving the private sector the maximum scope to respond and re-open quickly following a disaster not only helps the economy in some narrow sense but is also important for facilitating the reconstruction of social capital and community by providing physical sites of social interaction.

4.6   Conclusion

Emphasizing the private sector's important contributions to disaster relief does not necessarily imply that there is no role for government. Instead, the point is to counter the often-told tale that it is *only* government, and especially only the *federal* government, that can effectively respond to natural disasters. The history of disaster response, both recently and in the distant past, provides clear evidence of the private sector's important and effective role. As we think about public policy with respect to disaster response, this history needs to be part of the conversation. At the very least, government needs to adopt a "first, do no harm" policy by allowing the private sector to do the things it is capable of doing best without the public sector getting in the way. What the private sector does best should also not be limited to the narrowly economic, as getting stores re-opened is crucial to rebuilding social capital and a broader sense of community. No one wants another disaster of that scale, but if and when it happens, let's hope the lessons of Hurricanes Katrina and Harvey have been learned and that the variety of decentralized and bottom-up responders, especially the private sector, play a major role in disaster response.

Notes

1. My discussions of Hurricane Katrina draw heavily on Horwitz (2009) and the sources therein.
2. On the Loads of Hope program, see https://tide.com/en-us/about-tide/loads-of-hope/about-loads-of-hope.
3. For a more complete discussion of the way in which firms displayed a variety of the "bourgeois virtues" in their responses to Hurricane Katrina, see Horwitz (2010).
4. The Cajun Navy is slowly becoming more institutionalized, as is seen at their website at https://louisianacn.com/.
5. The argument of this paragraph is developed more completely in Horwitz (2018).
6. This section draws heavily from Horwitz (2010).

References

Coate, D. 2011. Disaster and Recovery: The Public and Private Sectors in the Aftermath of the 1906 Earthquake in San Francisco. *Journal of Critical Incident Analysis* 1 (2): n.p.

Edwards, C. 2017. Natural Disasters Before Big Government. *Cato at Liberty*, September 5. https://www.cato.org/blog/natural-disasters-big-government.

Hayek, F.A. 1945. The Use of Knowledge in Society. *The American Economic Review* 35 (4): 519–530.

———. 1989. *The Fatal Conceit: The Errors of Socialism*. Edited by W.W. Bartley III. Chicago: University of Chicago Press.

Horwitz, S. 2009. Wal-Mart to the Rescue: Private Enterprise's Response to Hurricane Katrina. *The Independent Review* 13 (4): 511–528.

———. 2010. Doing the Right Things: The Private Sector Response to Hurricane Katrina as a Case Study in the Bourgeois Virtues. In *Accepting the Invisible Hand: Market-Based Approaches to Social Economic Problems*, ed. M.D. White, 169–190. New York: Palgrave Macmillan.

———. 2016. In Natural Disasters, Companies Operate Like Neighbors. *Wall Street Journal*, June 7. https://www.wsj.com/articles/in-natural-disasters-companies-operate-like-neighbors-1465338881.

———. 2018. *Households as Crisis Shock Absorbers*. SSRN Working Paper No. 3259507. https://papers.ssrn.com/sol3/papers.cfm?abstract_id=3259507.

Perry, M. 2017. Private Sector to the Rescue in Texas. *Carpe Diem*, August 29. http://www.aei.org/publication/private-sector-to-the-rescue-never-underestimate-the-power-of-the-private-sector-to-rise-up-to-face-any-challenge/.

Rosengrant, S. 2007. *Wal-Mart's Response to Hurricane Katrina: Striving for a Public-Private Partnership*. Kennedy School of Government Case Program C16-07-1876.0. Cambridge, Harvard University, Kennedy School of Government.

Skarbek, E. 2014. The Chicago Fire of 1871: A Bottom-Up Approach to Disaster Relief. *Public Choice* 160 (1–2): 155–180.

Smith, D.J., and D. Sutter. 2013. Response and Recovery After the Joplin Tornado Lessons Applied and Lessons Learned. *The Independent Review* 18 (2): 165–188.

Storr, V.H. 2008. The Market as a Social Space: On the Meaningful Extraeconomic Conversations That Can Occur in Markets. *The Review of Austrian Economics* 21 (2–3): 135–150.

5

Formation of Public–Private Partnerships by Local Emergency Managers

Amy LePore

5.1 Introduction

Accountability for disaster management in the US has historically been centralized at the national level with most daily responsibilities assigned to local government emergency management outposts. While locally selected, the emergency manager is often funded by the federal government and is charged with the implementation of a framework intended to mirror federal efforts and to prepare jurisdictions for the receipt of federal assistance after disaster events. In 2010, due largely to the failures of this top-down model, the Federal Emergency Management Agency (FEMA) initiated its Whole Community doctrine, which elaborates on the necessity of nongovernmental entity involvement in disaster. After decades of reinforcing the message that FEMA was coming to the rescue, the "federal family" tacitly acknowledged what most already knew—government cannot and should not solely manage disasters. In an absurd

A. LePore (✉)
Anthem Planning, Inc., Middletown, DE, USA
e-mail: alepore@anthemplanning.com

© The Author(s) 2020   **71**
S. Haeffele, V. H. Storr (eds.), *Bottom-up Responses to Crisis*, Mercatus Studies
in Political and Social Economy, https://doi.org/10.1007/978-3-030-39312-0_5

turn of events, FEMA acted on this acknowledgment by dictating methods of reform to local emergency management offices. Emergency managers, armed with a top-down mandate, are now charged with instituting a bottom-up approach. The intergovernmental arrangements that permit this perversion of federalism are commonplace among federal, state, and local governments. The submissive nature of the local offices and their willingness to cede autonomy is a reflection of their need for federal support if they are to continue operating. In return for the federal favor, however, locals are assigned a set of tasks intended to disperse accountability across the sectors. The chapter proceeds as follow. Section 5.2 reviews the nature of these tasks, while Sect. 5.3 examines the potential challenges for the local emergency management offices to complete the federal dictum. Section 5.4 considers this arrangement in relation to federalism and its intended structures for intergovernmental relations. And, concluding thoughts are offered in Sect. 5.5.

5.2 Federal Guidance for Local Emergency Management

5.2.1 Whole Community

The context in which emergency managers have been asked to disperse accountability was provided for in FEMA's Whole Community doctrine. Whole Community was not the first effort of the federal government to attempt grassroots level reach. Project Impact, the most notable example, claimed community organizer status as well. Its stated effort, to "bring communities together to take actions that prepare for—and protect themselves against—natural disasters in a collaborative effort" (FEMA 1996, summary page), lasted as long as the federal funding. As a result, and as expected with federal intervention in local matters, "FEMA sought to circumvent state governments and work directly with localities" (Birkland and Waterman 2008, 698). As will be addressed in Sect. 5.3, perversions of federalism are commonplace in FEMA programs.

The Whole Community approach followed a series of attempts to reform and remold federal emergency management. It presented the new concept, however, that accountability for disasters should be shared after years of referencing FEMA as a "federal family" ready to rescue (O'Keefe 2011). The Whole Community approach has been the subject of several studies. Notably, FEMA commissioned its own study and enlisted the help of the CDC. The study's intention, to "identify, promote, and learn from examples of existing community efforts that exemplify a whole community approach to preparedness and emergency response for the purpose of informing potential, recommended methods for other communities," was carried out by federally funding seven programs and then using them as specimens of grassroots effort (Sobelson et al. 2015). Garrels-Bates (2018) further supported federally funded localism by opining that a primary purpose for the lack of utility of predecessor programs, such as Citizen Corps and Community Emergency Response Training, is due to insufficient federal funding. Another explanation for their failure, however, is the inability or unwillingness of local jurisdictions to absorb the cost of local efforts. In fact, in 2012, ten years after the program's inception, nearly 50 percent of Citizen Corps programs relied on at least 50 percent federal funding. Of these programs, 75 percent relied on 75 percent funding (FEMA 2012).

5.2.2 Public–Private Partnerships and the Collective Impact Model

As an outgrowth of FEMA's Whole Community approach, there has been a focus on partnerships with the private sector—presumably to piggyback on the success associated with effective business management and logistics in the post-disaster environment (Kapucu et al. 2010; Chandra et al. 2016). FEMA now provides a series of resources and training modules intended to be used by local emergency managers tasked with the establishment and maintenance of these partnerships.

The term "public–private partnerships" itself is offered a set of broad definitions as it refers to many forms of cross-sector relationships. In the case of this review of the literature, however, there is a specific focus on the formation of partnerships between public emergency management and the private sector. To that end, Bovaird (2004, 200) offers that public–private partnerships are "working arrangements based on a mutual commitment (over and above that implied in any contract) between a public sector organization with any organization outside of the public sector." Linder (1999) also outlines a multitude of types, the first "partnership as management reform" most closely parallels the nature of partnership that is encouraged by whole community efforts. In its admission of the problems with a federal-centric response, FEMA signaled to local emergency managers that they might, as Linder (1999, 42) points out, "change the way government functions, largely by tapping into the discipline of the market."

Collaboration between agencies involved in emergency management has been the focus of multiple studies (Caruson and MacManus 2012; McGuire and Silvia 2010). To enable emergency managers and their partners to capitalize on lessons learned, the FEMA course *Maturing Public Private Partnerships* was developed (Mid-Atlantic Center for Emergency Management 2018). In keeping with the Whole Community approach, it draws on the numerous collaborative efforts at lower levels intended to disperse responsibility for a broad swath of issues and specifically recommends the use of the collective impact model. Collective impact, the "commitment of a group of important actors from different sectors to a common agenda for solving a specific social problem," is an increasingly used approach that seeks to challenge the status quo isolation of agencies working in the social sector (Kania and Kramer 2011, 36). Done with fidelity, this model is implemented with five specific conditions. Those conditions include (1) the formation of a common agenda; (2) the use of the shared system of measurement; (3) the assurance that activities undertaken by the partners will be mutually reinforcing; (4) consistent communications; and (5) a backbone, or administrative, organization at the helm.

Kania and Kramer (2011) form the basis for the collective impact model, which stood as a call for the social sector to eliminate its silo-mentality, citing specific problems with this historical approach. They noted, "As a result of this process, nearly 1.4 million nonprofits try to invent independent solutions to major social problems, often working at odds with each other and exponentially increasing the perceived resources required to make meaningful progress" (Kania and Kramer 2011, 38). Progress has stalled previously, they posited, because organizations operate independently as opposed to using a more collaborative approach. Success, in Kania and Kramer's (2011, 41) opinion, would be a "new approach that will enable us to solve today's most serious social problems with the resources we already have at our disposal. It would be a shock to the system. But it's a form of shock therapy that's badly needed." Interestingly, the Kania and Kramer critique does not necessarily extend to government, but much the same can be said about duplicative program design and spending in the public sector. How can we be sure that collective impact is new or different from previously employed models of collaboration? Examples of the federal government "empowering" local entities to use funds and make grassroots decisions are plentiful. Few are as telling as the federal government's Social Innovation Fund (SIF)—yet another centralized effort that thwarts a local approach. Through the Corporation for National and Community Service, the federal government hand-selected non-profit entities to carry out federally sanctioned programming. A series of problems followed, including the hesitancy of large donors to get involved and the inability of the newly funded programs to raise matching funds. Howard Husock (2013, n.p.) observed,

> Perhaps donors are reluctant to participate because they realize that the SIF represents the politicization of private charity. Consider the donors that have provided matching funds. They include banks, health-care firms, and Freddie Mac, the government-backed housing enterprise—all deeply entwined with government regulators and with plenty of motivation to stay in the White House's good graces.

Again, despite claims that such programs restore funds to the local community, the process by which private charities are chosen by a national government subverts a local process. Even neighborhood-based work is sidelined and bureaucratized by the acceptance of federal funds. A GAO (2014, 21, 25) report on the much-celebrated Promise Neighborhoods program stated that it "has not developed an inventory of federal programs that could contribute to Promise program goals that it could share with planning and implementation grantees and use to make its own decisions about coordination across agencies," and "has not decided whether it will make the first year's data public because it was not collected in a consistent manner…."

Whole Community, Promise Neighborhoods, SIF, and many other similar programs are focused on the same type of next-level community collaboration that Kania and Kramer recommend. Yet the believers in the collective impact model, including FEMA, claim to have an improved process adept at breaking down silos and increasing accountability. If examples of success in employing this model in public–private partnerships for emergency management exist, they are not clearly demonstrated. Of the five model county partnerships offered by FEMA, none use the collective impact model (FEMA 2015). While each seems to be a forthright effort at information sharing with the private sector, all five are still typified by a government-as-leader and private sector-as-helper model. In fact, much of the language reinforces that the government must be at the helm. For example, the Victoria County, Texas Office of Emergency Management (Lacey 2015, 2) describes their public–private partnership as permission-based and notes that their approach is "rooted in a principle we have coined 'Strategic Disassociation,' we can allow certain groups to operate with limited or no involvement from the local government." It does not appear that these efforts are in the model of collective impact as described by Kania and Kramer.

The call for an increased level of cross-sector collaboration on disaster management issues should, by the very definition of the shared responsibility that accompanies the collective impact literature, advance the cause of the efficient use of local resources, reduce reliance on any one sector for solving problems, and decentralize financial responsibility. Shared goals and the elimination of redundancy should be the clear aims of such an initiative and would marry well with the effort to sustain local solutions. The local examples offered by FEMA do not demonstrate the recommended model so that we can assess their ability to align work and eliminate redundancy. What we can be sure of is that pre-Whole Community language, which places government in charge is alive and well in partnerships. The cautionary tale here is that models of collaboration as they are outlined in social science and authorized by the federal government are not always success stories. It remains to be seen how the collective impact model, recommended by FEMA, will perform better than previous interventions in local affairs.

5.3 Local Emergency Management Challenges

5.3.1 Centralization and Instability

After decades of intervention in local disaster management, the acknowledgment by FEMA that local-level community support is most effective came a bit late in the game. Increasing the accountability of individuals and organizations closest to a problem should have always been a broad cross-sector goal of any initiative that seeks to tackle emergency management issues. However, in forwarding the Whole Community doctrine, FEMA still fell short of admitting what scholars know. The result of a strong local role in problem solving of any sort, not just disaster-related, will be reduced government intervention from levels further from the problem (Donahue and Joyce 2001; Sankaran 2007; Mayer 2009). The potential benefits of decreasing far-removed intervention on local matters include reduced dependency and increased autonomy for decision making (Lovell 1981). Yet, despite these benefits and general agreement about local intervention efficacy, much of the responsibility for ameliorating social problems in the US is centralized at the national level (Yoo 2005; Kincaid and Cole 2008; Gais 2010). Centralization of the responsibility to pay and to conduct program design presents a direct challenge to effective local partnering. Emergency management is an excellent example of this, where general agreement exists among county emergency mangers that they cannot survive without FEMA (Crabill 2015). When asked about the impact of one particular funding source, the Emergency Management Performance Grant, most emergency managers in a 2015 study reported their inability to continue their work in its absence.[1] Many emergency managers shared their sentiments:

- "It funds the emergency management coordinator position within the county. Without the funding, I do not believe the County would keep the position."
- "Without it, we would be unable to function."
- "Without the EMPG, it is likely that we would not have an emergency management program in this county."

Underscoring the idea of unsustainable activity is the agreement by emergency managers themselves that their primary financial objective is to obtain federal funds. Crabill's (2015) survey demonstrated that only 37 percent of emergency managers applied for nonfederal funding, and only 3 percent had refused federal funds. This commitment to obtaining federal dollars is present despite their acknowledgment of lost autonomy. In the same survey, a majority of emergency managers reported that they had an insufficient level of autonomy from the federal government to make the best decisions possible for the local organization (Crabill 2015, 81). If there is not local financial stability or policy independence for emergency management offices, it must be considered if emergency management is best positioned to be the steward of local partnerships and distributor of accountability. Further, this instability is evidence of problematic intergovernmental relationships that will be addressed in Sect. 5.4.

5.3.2   Emergency Management Finances

Several additional challenges exist which can stall partnership formation. Historically, the matter of finances has presented several challenges to relationships between emergency management agencies and their partners. Choi and Kim (2007) point out that the amount of influence an emergency management office is perceived to have is directly related to their role as decision maker for funding streams. Conversely, according to the same study, an emergency manager's limited role as a recipient of funds garnered them far less influence. The challenge presented by finances is also evident in the disaster declaration process, which is tied to billions of available dollars and increasingly used as a tool of politics (Garrett and Sobel 2003; Sobel and Leeson 2006; Sylves and Búzás 2007). We often hear about mistakes made at the federal level, but the politicization of emergency management funding is most damaging at the local level. These problems often take a less visible form—a quiet compliance in return for funding that veers away from local needs and can thwart attempts at trusting local relationships. Donahue and Joyce (2001, 477) note that while local governments do share in the responsibility for response and recovery "they may modify their activities in these areas to conform to federal criteria to secure as many resources as possible." This type of activity is encouraged by the federal government, regardless of the general acknowledgment that financial and programmatic dependence is unhealthy for local governments (Lovell 1981; Birkland and Waterman 2008).

5.3.3 Emergency Management Skills

Further, because public and private sector motives are not in sync, the emergency manager must identify ways to navigate difficult relationships during partnership formation. The skill set required to form, maintain, and employ partnerships during disasters includes a considerable set of interpersonal and managerial skills (Waugh 1991; Waugh and Streib 2006). More importantly however, unleashing private assets in a way that benefits the whole community requires a basic understanding and appreciation of market principles. Can the emergency manager follow the recommendation of Horwitz (2008, 2) and help to "give the private sector as much freedom as possible to provide resources for relief and recovery efforts and ensure that its role is officially recognized as part of disaster protocols"? The oft competing motives of regulation and economic restoration may or may not be something an emergency manager is prepared to manage effectively. Consider the nature of challenges to private sector freedom that should be met by whole community partnerships in the post-disaster environment. Chamlee-Wright and Storr (2008) offer three examples: day care provider shortages, zoning restrictions, and occupational licensing requirements. Each of these challenges finds the public and private sectors at odds, but is absolutely and completely necessary to hasten community return and restoration of the economic base. It is important to understand if the average emergency manager is prepared to navigate partnerships to this type of success by assessing what competencies are expected of him. Feldmann-Jensen, Jensen, and Smith (2017) and the International Association of Emergency Managers (n.d.) have compiled lists of competencies that demonstrate attributes of a consensus-builder. However, neither set of competencies, despite FEMA's endorsement, includes market acumen.

Thus, at the helm of steering partnerships toward shared accountability is a captain that is subject to the rules and donations of the federal government and engaged in a local area where perceived power comes from ruling over disaster dollars. It is difficult to see how federally inspired local collaboration might proliferate in this environment.

5.4   Federal Emergency Management Guidance and Federalism

Greve (2000) posits that autonomy for state and local governments decreases as institutional collusion to secure federal resources increases. This move from competitive federalism, or a federalism that promotes competition between governments, and toward a cooperative model has a series of consequences that impact emergency management. Cooperation grants the federal government authority over the state and local policy space in exchange for grant funds and the ability to increase in size and scope. As Greve (2000, 570) points out, the granting of federal funds simply grows "intergovernmental bureaucracies and policy cartels at the state and local level." This growth comes at the cost of autonomy and in this case, an unprepared populace and an overly involved national government (Lovell 1981; Crabill and Rademacher 2012).

Greve (2000) cautioned against governments at the local and state levels cooperating to cede policy space and autonomy to the federal government in exchange for money. Instead of heeding this warning, lobbying efforts through the International Association of Emergency Managers and the National Emergency Management Association have placed an enormous amount of focus on increasing federal expenditures on local issues. In fact, both organizations name this increase as a priority (IAEM 2018; NEMA n.d.). The cooperation to plead for budget increases by local, state, and federal officials through these associations has, as Greve (2000, 558) warns, accommodated "political and interest group demands."

It is already established that intervention into local emergency management matters by the federal government has resulted in dependence for local offices. However, it is the long-term result of this dependence that Greve is concerned with. When funding a local program is not in the purview of a local government, neither is policy making or program design. Once the federal government is invited to make decisions on local issues for daily operations, there ceases to be control over what the federal government might do when crisis or conflict arises. We might look to emergency management's founding doctrine to understand the outermost limits of federal power. The Stafford Act states that when it is "necessary to save lives, prevent human suffering, or mitigate severe damage," it can deploy resources without state consent (FEMA 2016, 26). The Stafford Act also states that the necessity to communicate with the state "shall not, in notifying and coordinating with a State under subparagraph (A), delay or impede the rapid deployment, use, and distribution of critical resources to victims of an emergency" (FEMA 2016, 27).

It is important to consider what competitive federalism might have meant to emergency management. In such a scenario the decision to fund a program would be in the hands of local elected officials and not far-removed federal personnel. Their decision would be based on risk and community willingness to support such an office. Competitive federalism would offer scalable programs intended to meet risk, and the cost of that risk would be borne by program benefactors. Unfortunately, however, as Greve (2000, 559) points out "cooperative federalism cannot be justified as an effective or public-interested regime. Rather, it can only be understood as an accommodation to interest group demands and to the interests of imperfectly monitored political actors." What better way to reduce the ability of a populace to monitor programs than to hide their costs by distributing risk? A competitive model would increase monitoring capability by drawing a clear and relevant connection between local taxes and program efficacy.

5.5 Conclusion

While emergency management has increasingly been funded and designed by the federal government, FEMA activity since 2010 seems to indicate an acknowledgment of the fundamental flaws in a top-down system. The federal government has put forward the Whole Community initiative with a stated goal of dispersing accountability for disaster management activities. The locally positioned, but often federally supported, emergency managers face several considerable challenges in implementing this whole community approach. Many local emergency managers have admitted dependence on the federal government for keeping their office doors open. Despite the lack of autonomy that serves as the trade-off, emergency managers target federal funding as a primary means of sustenance. Thus, accountability is not yet shared by local governments that are supposed to further devolve disaster responsibilities to the community level. Additionally, emergency managers are not expected to understand how to negotiate differing sector motives nor how to play a support role to the private sector. While FEMA's preferred partnership model of collective impact has received notoriety in the social sector, examples of county collaborations offered by FEMA are not using it and in fact, those examples still read like command and control models.

All of these concerns with the suggested model, however, pale in comparison to the absurdity of federally mandated local approaches to partnership building. Such guidance could only be passed on by a centralized government that understood its role as primary payer and, as a result, program designer. This level of intervention is the direct result of agency, association, and government collusion to keep the federal funds coming at any cost. May no state ever realize the full cost of a strong, centralized government that is free to define disaster and ultimately, to dictate the response.

Note

1. An electronic survey was sent to 2339 county emergency managers during the Fall of 2013, with 598 respondents.

References

Birkland, T., and S. Waterman. 2008. Is Federalism the Reason for Policy Failure in Hurricane Katrina? *Publius: The Journal of Federalism* 38 (4): 692–714.

Bovaird, T. 2004. Public–Private Partnerships: From Contested Concepts to Prevalent Practice. *International Review of Administrative Sciences* 70 (2): 199–215.

Caruson, K., and S.A. MacManus. 2012. Interlocal Emergency Management Collaboration: Vertical and Horizontal Roadblocks. *Publius: The Journal of Federalism* 42 (1): 162–187.

Chamlee-Wright, E.L., and V.H. Storr. 2008. The Entrepreneur's Role in Post-Disaster Community Recovery: Implications for Post-Disaster Recovery Policy. *Mercatus Policy Series, Policy Primer No. 6*: 1–11. https://doi.org/10.2139/ssrn.1350513.

Chandra, A., S. Moen, and C. Sellers. 2016. What Role Does the Private Sector Have in Supporting Disaster Recovery, and What Challenges Does It Face in Doing So? *RAND Corporation Perspective*: 1–24. https://www.rand.org/pubs/perspectives/PE187.html.

Choi, S.O., and B.-T. Kim. 2007. Power and Cognitive Accuracy in Local Emergency Management Networks. *Public Administration Review* 67 (S1): 198–209.

Crabill, A.L. 2015. *The Effects of Federal Financial Assistance: Attitudes and Actions of Local Emergency Managers*. University of Delaware Thesis. http://udspace.udel.edu/handle/19716/17054.

Crabill, A.L., and Y. Rademacher. 2012. Breaking the Cycle of Reliance on Federal Help After Disasters. *Emergency Management Magazine*.

Donahue, A.K., and P.G. Joyce. 2001. A Framework for Analyzing Emergency Management with an Application to Federal Budgeting. *Public Administration Review* 61 (6): 728–740.

Feldmann-Jensen, S., S. Jensen, and S.M. Smith. 2017. *The Next Generation Core Competencies for Emergency Management Professionals: Handbook of Behavioral Anchors and Key Actions for Measurement*. Washington, DC: FEMA Higher

Education Program. https://training.fema.gov/hiedu/docs/emcompetencies/final_%20ngcc_and_measures_aug2017.pdf

FEMA. 1996. *The Project Impact Guidebook*. Washington, DC: Federal Emergency Management Agency. https://training.fema.gov/hiedu/docs/hazriskmanage/hazards%20risk%20mgmt%20-%20session%204%20-%20project%20impact%20guidebook.pdf

FEMA. 2012. *Citizen Corps Council Registration and Profile Data: FY2011 National Report*. Washington, DC: Federal Emergency Management Agency. https://s3-us-gov-west-1.amazonaws.com/dam-production/uploads/20130726-1854-25045-2121/citizen_corps_councils_final_report_9_27_2012.pdf

FEMA. 2015. Public Private Partnership Models. *FEMA.gov*. https://www.fema.gov/public-private-partnership-models.

FEMA. 2016. *Robert T. Stafford Disaster Relief and Emergency Assistance Act, as Amended, and Related Authorities as of August 2016, Public Law 93–288*. Washington, DC: Federal Emergency Management Agency. https://www.fema.gov/media-library/assets/documents/15271.

Gais, T.L. 2010. *Federalism During the Obama Administration*. Presented at the 27th Annual Conference of the National Federation of Municipal Analysts. https://rockinst.org/wp-content/uploads/2017/11/2010-05-07-federalism_during_obama_administration-min.pdf.

GAO. 2014. *Education Grants: Promise Neighborhoods Promotes Collaboration but Needs National Evaluation Plan*. US Government Accountability Office Report GAO-14-432, 1–55. https://www.gao.gov/products/gao-14-432.

Garrels-Bates, M. 2018. *Using the Fire Service to Build Community Engagement*. Naval Postgraduate School Thesis. https://www.hsdl.org/?view&did=811398.

Garrett, T.A., and R.S. Sobel. 2003. The Political Economy of FEMA Disaster Payments. *Economic Inquiry* 41 (3): 496–509.

Greve, M.S. 2000. Against Cooperative Federalism. *Mississippi Law Journal* 70 (2): 557–623.

Horwitz, S. 2008. Making Hurricane Response More Effective: Lessons from the Private Sector and the Coast Guard During Katrina. *Mercatus Policy Series, Policy Comment No. 17* (2008). https://papers.ssrn.com/abstract=1350554.

Husock, H. 2013. Politicizing Philanthropy: A White House Program Blurs the Line between Government Action and Private Charity. *City Journal* (Winter), n.p. https://www.city-journal.org/html/politicizing-philanthropy-13535.html.

IAEM. 2018. *IAEM-USA Legislative Priorities.* Falls Church, VA: US Council of International Association of Emergency Managers. http://www.iaem.com/documents/IAEM-Legislative-Priorities-Summer2018.pdf.

IAEM. n.d. *Emergency Management: Definition, Vision, Mission, Principles.* Falls Church, VA: US Council of International Association of Emergency Managers. http://www.iaem.com/documents/Principles-of-Emergency-Management-Flyer.pdf.

Kania, J., and M. Kramer. 2011. Collective Impact. *Stanford Social Innovation Review,* Winter, 36–41. https://ssir.org/articles/entry/collective_impact.

Kapucu, N., T. Arslan, and F. Demiroz. 2010. Collaborative Emergency Management and National Emergency Management Network. *Disaster Prevention and Management: An International Journal* 19 (4): 452–468.

Kincaid, J., and R.L. Cole. 2008. Public Opinion on Issues of Federalism in 2007: A Bush Plus? *Publius: The Journal of Federalism* 38 (3): 469–487.

Lacey, J.B. 2015. Victoria Partners in Preparedness. *FEMA.gov.* https://www.fema.gov/pdf/privatesector/ppp_victoria_county.pdf

Linder, S. 1999. Coming to Terms with the Public-Private Partnership; A Grammar of Multiple Meanings. *American Behavioral Scientist* 43 (1): 35–51.

Lovell, C.H. 1981. Evolving Local Government Dependency. *Public Administration Review* 41 (Special Issue: The Impact of Resource Scarcity on Urban Public Finance): 189–202.

Mayer, M. 2009. States: Stop Subsidizing FEMA Waste and Manage Your Own Local Disasters. *The Heritage Foundation Backgrounder No. 2323,* 1–9. https://www.heritage.org/homeland-security/report/states-stop-subsidizing-fema-waste-and-manage-your-own-local-disasters.

McGuire, M., and C. Silvia. 2010. The Effect of Problem Severity, Managerial and Organizational Capacity, and Agency Structure on Intergovernmental Collaboration: Evidence from Local Emergency Management. *Public Administration Review* 70 (2): 279–288.

Mid-Atlantic Center for Emergency Management at Frederick Community College. 2018. Maturing Public-Private Partnerships Workshops. Frederick, MD: Mid-Atlantic Center for Emergency Management. https://macematfcc.wordpress.com/category/p3/.

NEMA. n.d. NEMA's Role in Washington. *National Emergency Management Association,* n.p. https://www.nemaweb.org/index.php?option=com_content&view=article&id=220&Itemid=402.

O'Keefe, E. 2011. Origins of the 'Federal Family.' *The Washington Post,* August 29, Washington D.C.: https://www.washingtonpost.com/blogs/federal-eye/

post/origins-of-the-federal-family/2011/08/29/gIQALov8mJ_blog.html?noredirect=on&utm_term=.e16cbb41d04b.

Sankaran, V. 2007. Innovation Held Hostage: Has Federal Intervention Stifled Efforts to Reform the Child Welfare System? *University of Michigan Journal of Law Reform* 41 (1): 281–315.

Sobel, R.S., and P.T. Leeson. 2006. Government's Response to Hurricane Katrina: A Public Choice Analysis. *Public Choice* 127 (1–2): 55–73.

Sobelson, R.K., C.J. Wigington, V. Harp, and B.B. Bronson. 2015. A Whole Community Approach to Emergency Management: Strategies and Best Practices of Seven Community Programs. *Journal of Emergency Management* 13 (4): 349–357. https://www.ncbi.nlm.nih.gov/pmc/articles/PMC5582971/.

Sylves, R., and Z.I. Búzás. 2007. Presidential Disaster Declaration Decisions, 1953–2003: What Influences Odds of Approval? *State and Local Government Review* 39 (1): 3–15.

Waugh, W.L. 1991. *Coordination or Control: Organizational Design and the Emergency Management Function.* Presented at the UCLA International Conference on the Impact of Natural Disasters, University of California, Los Angeles. http://65.182.2.242/docum/crid/Septiembre-Octubre2005/CD-1/pdf/eng/doc6414/doc6414-contenido.pdf.

Waugh, W.L., and G. Streib. 2006. Collaboration and Leadership for Effective Emergency Management. *Public Administration Review* 66 (s1): 131–140.

Yoo, J. 2005. What Became of Federalism? *Los Angeles Times,* June 21, n.p. http://articles.latimes.com/2005/jun/21/opinion/oe-yoo21.

6

Children Take Charge: Helping Behaviors and Organized Action Among Young People After Hurricane Katrina

Lori Peek, Jessica Austin, Elizabeth Bittel, Simone Domingue, and Melissa Villarreal

6.1 Prologue

Oronde[1] was 11 years old when Hurricane Katrina devastated the U.S. Gulf Coast. He, like tens of thousands of other children, evacuated and was displaced from his native New Orleans. Oronde experienced much uncertainty and ongoing academic disruption as his family sought safe and stable housing in the years after the storm.

After several moves across Louisiana and Texas, he, his mother, and his younger siblings returned to the changed physical and social environment they and many others dubbed "the new New Orleans." Like a boat adrift,

---

The second, third, fourth, and fifth authors are listed in alphabetical order to denote equal contributions to this chapter. The authors would like to thank Stefanie Haeffele and Virgil Henry Storr at the Mercatus Center at George Mason University for their editorial leadership. John Boyne, while a master's student at Colorado State University, and Nicole Mattson, while an undergraduate student at the University of Colorado Boulder, assisted with the data collection and analyses for this chapter. Allison Carlock, National Youth Preparedness Lead at the Federal Emergency Management Agency, reviewed an earlier draft of this chapter, which is gratefully acknowledged. *This material is based upon work supported by the National Science Foundation under grant no. 1635593. Any opinions, findings, and conclusions or recommendations expressed in this material are those of the authors and do not necessarily reflect the views of the National Science Foundation.*

© The Author(s) 2020
S. Haeffele, V. H. Storr (eds.), *Bottom-up Responses to Crisis*, Mercatus Studies in Political and Social Economy, https://doi.org/10.1007/978-3-030-39312-0_6

Oronde sought stability—an anchor—after the storm. His crumbling school, which was in receivership by the state before Katrina, was shuttered permanently following the catastrophe. The New Orleans charter school where his mother finally enrolled him in 2007, two years after Katrina's floodwaters laid waste to an already failing system, had been repaired but was badly under-resourced and staffed by a team of inexperienced educators fresh out of college.

As Oronde attempted to adjust to the new classroom environment, new peers, new teachers, a different rental home, and a radically changed neighborhood, he was introduced to Kids Rethink New Orleans Schools. Formed in 2006, the Rethinkers came together, with the support of adults, to ensure that young people's voices would be heard as decisions were being made regarding the New Orleans public school system. Over the years, the organization, which is now known simply as Rethink, has morphed into a group concerned with social, political, and economic justice to advance current and future prospects for youth of color in New Orleans and beyond.[2]

Soon after the group was formed, the Rethinkers decided that they would work together to identify one major issue that they wanted to tackle each year. The organizational model encourages youth voice and grassroots leadership to recognize, understand, and ultimately address issues of particular concern to young people. Using various creative means, the youth then tell the story of the grand challenges they face and

L. Peek (✉) • J. Austin • S. Domingue • M. Villarreal
Department of Sociology, University of Colorado Boulder, Boulder, CO, USA

Natural Hazards Center, University of Colorado Boulder, Boulder, CO, USA
e-mail: Lori.Peek@colorado.edu; Jess.Austin@colorado.edu;
Simone.Domingue@colorado.edu; Melissa.Villarreal@colorado.edu

E. Bittel
Department of Sociology, SUNY Cortland, Cortland, NY, USA

South Asia Program, Cornell University, Ithaca, NY, USA
e-mail: Elizabeth.Bittel@cortland.edu

offer concrete possibilities and actionable steps for change. They also learn lessons in how to work with hierarchical organizations and adult leaders to promote bottom-up, youth-initiated change.

Oronde and fellow Rethinkers staged a public event at a local community garden in the spring of 2011. There, they offered a presentation to the New Orleans superintendent of schools and leadership from the corporate food giant Aramark regarding the problems associated with the lack of fresh food in cafeterias throughout the city. The event, which was completely youth-led, involved presentations from Pre-Thinkers (younger, elementary school-age members of Rethink) as well as the Rethinkers. They addressed food issues in school cafeterias and explained how the lack of access to good food can influence learning outcomes. They then offered a clear plan for how to get more fruits and vegetables onto the lunch trays of schoolchildren. At the close of the session, the adult administrators agreed to sign off on the Rethinkers' demands for healthier and more environmentally sustainable food options.

After the event ended, Oronde shared more about his personal journey from displaced Katrina kid to local youth activist for school justice. Although he had always been a quiet and shy child, Rethink had "pushed him out of his comfort zone" and encouraged him to "find his voice" until he "realized what a difference" he and other children and youth could make. Through his involvement in Rethink, Oronde connected with supportive peers and adults, learned invaluable leadership skills, and came to recognize that youth can enact transformative change, even in the face of what may seem like insurmountable problems. His volunteerism through Rethink became a centerpiece of his college application essays, and he was proud to share with others that he had been accepted to college and would be studying mechanical engineering at the University of Mississippi in the fall of 2011.

Six years after Katrina upended nearly everything in his life, he said he was "recovered" and "ready" to continue on the path of scholarship and social change. He also observed that one of the biggest lessons he would take from his time in Rethink was the recognition of "exactly how much power youth can have when they unite."

6.2   Introduction

What do children do for themselves and for others in disasters? This is one of the core questions posed by Anderson (2005) in a foundational article calling for more social science investigations regarding the vulnerabilities and capacities of children and youth. Anderson argues that children "are not just passive in the face of disasters," nor are they "merely victims and dependent observers of the scene" (Anderson 2005, 168). Although he acknowledges throughout his writing that children and youth often lack power because they do not vote, and authority because they are typically excluded from decision-making bodies, he also notes that they undoubtedly contribute across the disaster lifecycle in terms of risk communication, preparedness, response, recovery, and mitigation.

In the years since that article was published, social scientists have responded to Anderson's call to document what children do before, during, and after disaster. In a 2008 special issue on children and disasters in the journal *Children, Youth and Environments*, several of the papers focused on children's active contributions to preparedness, response, and recovery.[3] Peek summarized those contributions and a number of case studies from around the world and observed that children have "considerable strengths that could serve as a significant resource for families, communities, and organizations attempting to prepare for, respond to, and recover from disasters" (Peek 2008, 14). Further, she argues that children's "knowledge, creativity, energy, enthusiasm, and social networks could be utilized during all phases of the disaster life cycle" (Peek 2008, 14) and advocates for more evidence from the field to document these actions. Towers et al. (2014) make a compelling case for acknowledging children's understanding of risk and strengthening children's skill sets to respond to a wide range of threats they may face in their environments. Moreover, a growing chorus of scholars from around the world has asserted that it is imperative that agencies and organizations democratize disaster risk reduction efforts by engaging children and youth as "experts" of their own environments and, in turn, calling on their unique knowledge and life experiences in all disaster planning efforts (Bartlett 2008; Back et al. 2009; Martin 2010; Haynes and Tanner 2015).

Heeding these calls, and drawing on nearly a decade of ethnographic fieldwork following Hurricane Katrina, Fothergill and Peek (2015) offer a typology of activities that affected children engaged in to help adults, other children and youth, and themselves both before and in the long-term aftermath of the catastrophe. They include evidence from interviews and observations that demonstrates that children did myriad things like assisting with evacuation preparations, rescuing other children and adults from the floodwaters, and educating and entertaining younger siblings and children while in shelters and temporary housing. This work underscores that children have special "talents, skills, and strengths" that can ultimately speed their own recovery and the recovery of those around them, after even the most disruptive of disasters (Fothergill and Peek 2015, 206).

Additional evidence suggests that children and youth may serve as active risk communicators, even helping adults to overcome language barriers during emergency response and initial phases of recovery (Back et al. 2009; Mitchell et al. 2008; Tanner 2010). Moreover, when engaged as key stakeholders within their communities rather than as token participants (Martin 2010), children have demonstrated their power as agents of change in disaster risk reduction (Mitchell et al. 2009) and climate change adaptation (Back et al. 2009; Tanner 2010) in low-income and developing countries.

Participatory action research (Haynes and Tanner 2015) has documented how children serve as advocates for climate change awareness and adaptation strategies in their community and how they contribute to citizen science initiatives regarding changing environmental conditions (Marchezini and Trajber 2017). For example, in the Philippines, children successfully campaigned for and initiated a community-wide referendum on school relocation when they learned their school was extremely vulnerable to landslide hazards (Back et al. 2009). Other participatory projects in the US and Canada have demonstrated the importance of engaging youth through creative means in telling their own stories of recovery, to ensure that their unique post-disaster needs are not overlooked in the adult-led recovery and reconstruction process (Fletcher et al. 2016; Peek et al. 2016)

Researchers have offered various explanations for children's effectiveness in assisting with and leading disaster risk reduction efforts. Back, Cameron, and Tanner (2009, 30), for instance, observe that in comparison to their adult counterparts, children and youth tend to be less fatalistic thinkers and employ a more "'yes we can' outlook," thereby opening pathways to creative and innovative solutions to socio-environmental problems. Additionally, Haynes and Tanner (2015) found that children and youth can more readily accept the social causes and consequences of disasters than adults, and as such have more malleable and adaptive ways of thinking that can serve them well in generating creative approaches to risk reduction. Indeed, Haynes and Tanner conclude that this malleable meaning-making capacity among youth makes them especially well positioned "to imagine, plan, and advocate for resilient futures" (Haynes and Tanner 2015, 367).

Researchers and practitioners alike agree that one of the first steps toward breaking down the barriers to children's participation is to flip the script on trust. This means adults must learn to recognize and encourage children as agentic thinkers and actors who are capable of constructive participation. This entails seeing children as active contributors to the processes of envisioning and manifesting solutions to socio-environmental problems at local, national, and global scales (Bartlett 2008; Back et al. 2009; Haynes and Tanner 2015).

Despite the rapidly growing body of literature that clearly documents children's capacities in disaster, children still tend to be regarded as unfit to participate in civil society (Jeffrey 2011; Lopez et al. 2012). They are often considered dependent on adults for guidance and viewed as not having the requisite skills or expertise for effective leadership or collective problem-solving. In some contexts, children are not given the right to engage in civil society and exercise their political will due to structural or procedural barriers imposed by adults (Lopez et al. 2012). Yet because children make up somewhere between one-quarter to one-half of the population of nations around the world (Bartlett 2008), and because they represent the future of all nations, it is crucial that scholars continue to document children's actions and contributions.

In this chapter, we take the position that children and youth—here defined as those under the age of 18—are capable actors who have the potential to actively contribute across the disaster lifecycle. Accordingly, we offer an analysis of children's helping behaviors following Hurricane

Katrina. Our project examines the helping behaviors of individual children and of groups, focusing attention to how young people engage in bottom-up responses even when they are not directly affected by a disaster. Drawing from a unique dataset of media coverage of children's helping behaviors, we argue that in addition to recognizing the strengths and capacities of disaster-affected children, children should also be recognized for their role as leaders in bottom-up responses to disaster. That is, not only are children reacting to their immediate circumstances, but they are also contributing to a broader civic response to crisis and are bringing to the table valuable, innovative, and forward-thinking ideas for how communities around the world can more effectively plan for and recover from disasters.

6.3 Approach

This chapter draws on a dataset that we generated of media coverage of children's helping behaviors in the aftermath of Hurricane Katrina.[4] Although prior studies of children in Katrina have focused on what the youngest survivors did to help others (Fothergill and Peek 2015; Mitchell et al. 2008), less is known about how children outside the disaster zone who were not directly affected contributed to the response and recovery.

In response to this gap in knowledge and our curiosity regarding how the media covers children's helping behaviors, we examined 108 news articles published in the ten-year period following Hurricane Katrina (2005–2015) that we identified through a LexisNexis database search. We used a combination of search terms including "children," "youth," "volunteer," "help," "disaster," "catastrophe," "Hurricane Katrina," and "Katrina" to find the articles.

After completing our initial search and downloading all of the returns, we reviewed each piece and deleted all duplicate entries and all non-relevant articles. We maintained all relevant news articles that were available via LexisNexis and published in the decade following Katrina in local, regional, and national newspapers. The majority of the articles (57 percent) were published in 2005, the year of the event, and 28 percent of the articles appeared in print over the next two years. Very few articles have been published in subsequent years (see Fig. 6.1).

Once we had identified the final set of news articles for analysis, we entered the bibliographic information into an Excel spreadsheet. We then

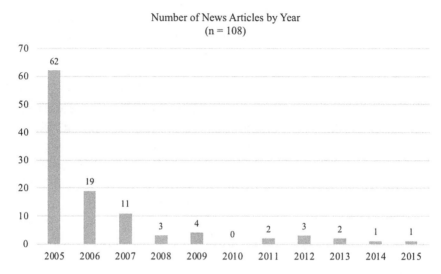

Fig. 6.1 Number of news articles focused on children's helping behaviors by year. (Source: Authors' creation)

developed additional columns to organize and analyze the entries along a number of dimensions that responded to calls for more information on children's helping behaviors in disaster (see Table 6.1). Three of the authors of the present chapter and a graduate research assistant read and categorized the articles along each dimension. Our initial inter-coder reliability was high, and we regularly met to cross-check and resolve any coding discrepancies.

6.4   Children's Helping Behaviors after Hurricane Katrina

Hurricane Katrina made landfall on August 29, 2005. The storm and the flooding that followed killed over 1800 people, destroyed hundreds of thousands of homes, resulted in economic damages in excess of $150 billion, and led to the evacuation of well over one million Gulf Coast residents (Rivlin 2015). Katrina still stands as one of the costliest and deadliest disasters in modern US history, and the storm laid bare many of the deep and abiding racial and economic divisions that mark our society during non-disaster times (Storr et al. 2015).

Table 6.1 Categories of analysis of children's helping behaviors

Location of the children helping/ where the helping occurred	Disaster phase when the helping occurred (emergency response, short-term recovery, long-term recovery)	Age(s) of children who engaged in helping behavior	Type(s) of help provided	Organization(s) that the children were involved with, if relevant	Organization(s) that the children were contributing to, if relevant	Tangible outcomes or change generated

Source: Authors' creation

Dramatic and devastating images of babies being rescued from rooftops, of children wading through neck-deep waters, and of thousands of Americans—most of them black and poor—trapped in desperate conditions at the Superdome in the city of New Orleans shocked and catalyzed many into action. Some came by rescue boat to try to help move people from the flooded city to higher ground. Others donated blood or gave cash contributions to local and national charities. Celebrities held benefit concerts and other events to raise additional funds for the survivors scattered far and wide across the nation.

As our analyses show, children also sprang into action after the storm. For some of the youngest helpers, this was the first major disaster that they had witnessed unfold in real time on their home television screens. For older youth, the imprint of the 9/11 tragedy, which also entailed a large number of deaths and concentrated destruction, was still fresh enough to remind them that they were coming of age in an era now regularly punctuated by catastrophe. Although children's precise motivation for helping was not always clear in the news articles that we reviewed, we were able to ascertain a range of things that children did to help in response to Hurricane Katrina.

6.4.1   How Did Children Help?

Our analyses revealed that the media covered six primary ways that children helped after Katrina (see Table 6.2): (1) raising money (43 percent); (2) collecting material goods for children and adult survivors (33 percent);

Table 6.2 Types of help children provided

Type of help	Number of articles[a]
Donating and raising money	57
Collecting and donating material goods and supplies	45
Necessities	22
Comfort goods	23
Assisting with restoration or rebuilding activities	18
Supporting mental health and raising spirits	6
Developing programs and raising awareness	5
Founding new organizations	3

Source: Authors' creation

[a]The total exceeds 108 as some articles mentioned more than one helping behavior or type of help provided

(3) developing programs to raise awareness of the disaster (4 percent); (4) assisting with restoration or rebuilding activities (13 percent); (5) raising spirits and mental health considerations (5 percent); and (6) creating new organizations to help with Katrina and future disasters (2 percent). We describe each of these activities briefly, drawing on the ways that the media covered children's helping behaviors.

6.4.1.1 Donating and Raising Money

Children as young as three years of age and through their late teens did many things to raise money after Katrina. Some literally emptied their piggy banks and sent the funds to affected schools or to national organizations such as the Salvation Army. In response to a national call from the American Red Cross, children from across the United States set up lemonade stands and sold drinks so they could donate the proceeds to Katrina relief (Vanden Brook 2005). In addition, school-age children across the US held bake sales and organized car washes and other events to raise cash contributions for Katrina survivors.

Children also created things so that they could sell products and donate the funds to disaster relief. For instance, one little girl made fans out of paper, sold them for $1 each, and donated all the profits to Katrina relief (Wiggins 2007). Other children made and sold bracelets (Sloan 2005), while another group of school children, who had also been involved after the 2004 Indian Ocean Earthquake and Tsunami, created a picture book that they sold and then donated all proceeds (Moore 2006).

6.4.1.2 Collecting and Donating Material Goods and Supplies

Disaster researchers have long discouraged the donation of goods and supplies after a catastrophe because research has repeatedly shown that such material convergence can create a disaster of its own (Phillips 2009). After Katrina, however, calls went out for toys, backpacks, warm clothing, and other items that children and families who had lost everything needed immediately and would need as the summer stretched into fall and winter.

Children across the nation responded to these calls through collecting both new and lightly used supplies and preparing them to be sent to the Gulf Coast. Children donated both comfort goods, which we defined as things like toys, stuffed animals, sports equipment, and leisure books, and basic necessities, such as food, water, clothing, school supplies, and toiletries. School classes collected backpacks and stuffed them with school supplies (Florida Times Union 2005). Children in northern states gathered up warmer winter clothes and blankets for Katrina survivors who were now scattered across the United States, and for many, living in colder climates for the first time (Peek and Richardson 2010). In addition to donating and gathering donated goods, a few of the news articles emphasized that children joined in-person distribution of the supplies along the Gulf Coast.

6.4.1.3   Assisting with Restoration and Rebuilding Activities

Of the news stories that focused on efforts to rebuild and restore badly damaged built and natural environments, nearly all focused on high school–age youth who, through their schools or places of worship, raised funds to travel to the Gulf Coast so they could provide direct assistance. These older youth engaged in a variety of short-term recovery activities associated with mucking out flooded homes, schools, churches, and other structures. Older youth also became involved in longer-term projects associated with restoring the wetlands and rebuilding homes and other structures that had been partially or completely damaged in the disaster. Several stories also focused on children's efforts to help rebuild child-centric spaces including playgrounds (Wiggins 2007), parks (Livingstone 2006), and school gardens (DeFour 2011).

6.4.1.4   Supporting Mental Health and Raising Spirits

Many children focused their efforts on improving the emotional status and raising the spirits of child and adult survivors of the storm. For example, children sent cards and letters of encouragement to affected individuals, many of whom had been displaced from their homes. Some children sent artwork. One child hosted a Christmas party for children in a FEMA trailer park (Frazier 2007), and a group of teenagers organized a vacation for affected teenagers in New Orleans, bringing 22 teens to Florida for a five-day winter vacation (Weingarten 2007).

6.4.1.5 Developing Programs and Raising Awareness

Children, like many adults, were obviously deeply moved by the images of profound human suffering that were so apparent in Hurricane Katrina. In response, children engaged in efforts to raise awareness of the extent of the physical and social damages caused by the storm. Young people hosted educational and benefit events that focused explicitly on the racial and class dimensions of the disaster and emphasized the long road to recovery ahead. One child created a mosaic in her community to draw attention to the plight of Katrina survivors (Javid-Yazdi 2007). Other children engaged fellow youth in listening activities in their schools and broader communities.

6.4.1.6 Creating New Organizations

Although much of the news coverage focused on heartfelt stories of individual children or on the efforts of a small group, it was also readily apparent that children and youth were working for more systemic and institutional change after Katrina. Indeed, a handful of news stories covered newly developed, youth-led grassroots organizations that were formed after the storm. Specifically, the coverage we reviewed focused on three organizations created by children to help with Katrina and any future disasters: RandomKid, a nonprofit focused on empowering "any random kid to solve real problems" (RandomKid 2010, n.p.); Kid4Kid, a nonprofit where "every child is important and can make a difference" (Kid4Kid 2017, n.p.); and Kids To The Rescue, formed to help kids to "learn the value of giving, not just in times of disaster like Katrina but as part of our everyday life" (Kids To The Rescue 2017, n.p.). All three of these organizations are still active today. And it is worth noting that there were many other youth-led groups that were created after Katrina (see Abramson et al. 2014; Fothergill and Peek 2015), which did not appear in the news coverage that we analyzed. What was clear in the analyses of this category of news coverage was that children and youth were attempting to bring fellow young people together to enact social or environmental change for the greater good.

6.4.2 How Old Were the Children Who Helped?

The news stories reviewed the actions of children as young as three years of age, to those who were in their late teens and graduating high school. Specifically, of the 108 articles, 34 (31 percent) focused on children of middle childhood (ages 6–11), 28 (26 percent) focused on teenagers (ages 15–17), and 17 (16 percent) focused on young teens (ages 12–14). Preschool children (ages 3–5) represented 5 percent of the sample, while children of multiple age groups represented 18 percent, and 4 percent of the articles did not specify an age (see Table 6.3).

6.4.3 Where Were the Children Who Helped and Who Were They Affiliated With?

The news stories we reviewed identified various states where children who sent help to hurricane-affected areas were located. Of the 108 articles, 16 described children's efforts from Florida, 12 from California, nine from Pennsylvania, and eight from Illinois. Most of the rest of the articles depicted children's help from various locations across the United States (see Table 6.4). Interestingly, four of the articles represented efforts among children in Canada, but no other foreign nations were mentioned in the media that we analyzed.

Table 6.3 Ages of children engaged in helping behaviors

Age group	Number of articles
Preschool (3–5)	5
Middle childhood (6–11)	34
Young teens (12–14)	17
Teenagers (15–17)	28
Multiple age groups	20
Not specified	4

Source: Authors' creation

Table 6.4 Number of articles by state where remote helping efforts were initiated

Location	Number of articles
Florida	16
California	12
Pennsylvania	9
Illinois	8
Multiple locations across the United States	3
Maine	3
Virginia, Massachusetts, Indiana, Georgia, Canada	4 articles each
Maryland, Iowa, Alabama, Ohio, Washington, Oklahoma, Missouri, Minnesota	2 articles each
Utah, New Jersey, South Dakota, Idaho, Texas, New York	1 article each

Source: Authors' creation

Some of the news coverage focused on children and youth traveling from outside the hurricane-affected region to Louisiana and Mississippi to provide hands-on help. Of the news articles we reviewed, nine described the efforts of children who traveled to New Orleans to help and six described children who went to Mississippi to help.

The post-Katrina news coverage that we analyzed focused on the activities of individual children as well as on classes, schools, and organized groups of children and youth who helped after the storm. Over half of the articles (53 percent) focused on schoolchildren and how they worked through their schools or school districts to help provide relief. The rest of the articles mentioned churches and youth groups (8 percent), nonprofits (7 percent), or children's own organizations (2 percent) as organizations that the children were affiliated with. In addition, three children (3 percent) represented organizations that do not fit into the aforementioned categories. These included a hospital, an ambulance company, and a government organization. The rest (27 percent) were not specified or not applicable—for instance, some children raised money individually (see Table 6.5).

6.4.4   When Did Children Help?

As noted previously, most of the articles we reviewed were published in the immediate aftermath of Katrina or in the first few years following the storm. Accordingly, coverage focused on what children were doing to

Table 6.5 Types of organizations children represented

Organization type	Number of articles[a]
School/school district	59
None specified/not applicable	30
Church/youth group	9
Nonprofit	8
Own organization	3
Other	3

Source: Authors' creation
[a]The total exceeds 108 as some articles mentioned more than one organization

assist in terms of initial emergency response versus short- or longer-term recovery efforts. Emergency response, which represents 43 percent of when children's helping behaviors took place, includes those actions and activities that occurred anywhere from zero to less than six weeks after the event. Short-term response, representing 31 percent of the articles, includes those where the helping occurred anywhere from six weeks up to one year after the event, as well as those that were written in 2005, but did not specify an exact time frame. Long-term response, encompassing 20 percent of articles, includes those where the helping occurred one year or longer after the event. Six articles, or 6 percent, did not specify when the helping occurred (see Fig. 6.2).

6.4.5   Which Organizations Did Children Contribute To?

While the majority of articles (51 percent) did not specify an organization that children contributed to, 38 (34 percent) named nonprofit/community-based organizations; of those donations, 65.8 percent were to the Red Cross. The rest of the articles mentioned schools (5 percent), relief funds (3 percent), children's own organizations (3 percent), and churches/youth groups (2 percent) as the types of organizations that the children contributed to. In addition, 3 percent of the articles described contributions to organizations that do not fit into the aforementioned categories, including FEMA, Scholastic Book Clubs, and an unincorporated volunteer group (see Table 6.6).

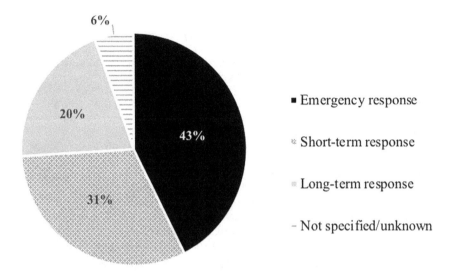

Fig. 6.2 Disaster phase when helping occurred. (Source: Authors' creation)

Table 6.6 Types of organizations children contributed to

Organization type	Number of articles[a]
None specified/not applicable	57
Nonprofit	38
School/school district	6
Relief funds	3
Own organization	3
Other	3
Church/youth group	1

Source: Authors' creation
[a]The total exceeds 108 as some articles mentioned more than one organization

6.4.6 A Sum Total of Children's Contributions

We concluded our analyses of the news coverage by attempting to sum up the tangible outcomes that resulted from children's post-Katrina helping efforts and their bottom-up organizing activities. Table 6.7 lists the things that children generated for others—which as previously discussed,

Table 6.7 Outcomes produced

Outcome	Details
Financial contributions	Over $471 million was raised
School supplies	Approximately 50,700 backpacks, plus 90 boxes full of backpacks; approximately 700 backpacks' worth of school supplies, plus $2000 worth of supplies
Books	23,000 books plus 400 "reading kits"
Toys	14,351 toys, plus 45 boxes' worth, $6000 generated for toys, and 170 "fun boxes" (kits with toys and other entertainment)
Necessities	200 toiletry kits; trailer full of bottled water; 2 truckloads of clothing; 500 hams for holidays; 2000 meals; 130 bricks for rebuilding
Labor power	Manual labor, including contributing to rebuilding efforts, cleaning/clearing debris, distributing supplies, and helping plant food gardens
Volunteer hours and other non-material contributions	Time spent with/reading to children and families; cards and letters to children; vacation for affected teenagers; Christmas party for children living in FEMA trailers

Source: Authors' creation

included raising money and collecting school supplies, books, toys, and other basic necessities (food, water, clothing, shelter, and toiletries)—as well as contributing labor and other services, such as reading to children and providing consolation.

According to our analyses, in terms of monetary assistance, children donated or raised over $471 million dollars after Katrina. School supplies were a common donation that children helped garner for Katrina survivors; the articles we reviewed described a total of 50,700 backpacks, plus 90 boxes full of backpacks, along with 700 backpacks full of supplies, and $2000 worth of school supplies gathered by children and youth. Children helped generate over 14,000 toy donations, plus 45 boxes full of toys, $6000 worth of toys, and 170 entertainment kits assembled by one school (Hussey 2005). Children organized the collection of over 23,000 new and used books and 400 new reading kits (DeFour 2011) after Katrina. Necessities offered included 200 toiletry kits (Kilbride 2005), a trailer full of bottled water, two truckloads of clothing, 500 hams for the holidays (Frazier 2007), 2000 meals, and 130 bricks for rebuilding (Smith 2006).

Children did much more than collect and distribute material donations, however. They also gave of their labor and time. Of the articles reviewed, 18 described children volunteering their labor to help with rebuilding efforts, cleaning and clearing debris, distributing supplies, and planting food gardens. Children also engaged in extensive volunteer efforts after the storm, including helping to raise people's spirits by creating artwork to send to children in affected areas (Averill 2005); sending cards and letters to children (Johnson 2005; Ramirez 2005; Cho 2005); organizing a short vacation for affected teenagers (Weingarten 2007); and planning a Christmas party for children living in FEMA trailers (Frazier 2007).

We categorized articles that specified a total monetary donation, results of a fundraising effort, or listed the number of goods donated by outcome and then added the totals together to give an overall sense of what children did after Katrina. Of course, this is an incomplete listing as we were only able to draw on the coverage available to us, and we know from our own research and experiences after Katrina that children did far more than was captured in these 108 news articles. Nevertheless, the sum total of what was covered by the media and summarized in Table 6.7 was still impressive in quantity and quality.

6.5 Conclusion

This chapter builds upon a growing body of literature that clearly demonstrates that children are highly capable and creative in the face of disaster (see Peek et al. 2018 for a recent review of this wave of research activity). Drawing on a dataset of news coverage of children's helping behaviors after Katrina, our analyses demonstrate how non-disaster affected children across the US contributed to post-Katrina response and recovery efforts. We found that children from age three onward did a range of things including making personal monetary donations and raising financial contributions, gathering necessary supplies and other goods, assisting with cleanup and rebuilding efforts, and otherwise working to improve present and future conditions for children and adults of the Gulf Coast.

While some of the activities that the children engaged in are conventional in that they mirror forms of help that adults often offer after disaster, these analyses demonstrate that children also can take charge after disaster. Children engaged in various child-centered helping behaviors including donating and gathering up various items that they knew would be meaningful to those of their same age range. They also collectively acted to educate and engage others in bottom-up collective organizing for social change. Perhaps most importantly, these stories demonstrate that children can and do make a real and potentially lasting difference after disaster. Further, this underscores why children should be treated as active agents, not as passive or uninterested observers (Pugh 2014).

At the same time, children are not isolated or acting independently most of the time. Indeed, our review of the media coverage showed that children often initiated helping behaviors, but they were also embedded within schools, churches, nonprofits, and other organizations that helped facilitated their post-disaster helping behaviors. In addition, often times children's help was geared toward supporting already-established or newly emergent organizations.

We argue that understanding children's helping behaviors—including those emergent or spontaneous behaviors as well as ones encouraged within organizational contexts—has important implications for how disaster resilience is fostered at a grassroots level. Just as adults regularly express a desire to help after a disaster (and disappointment when they are not allowed to do so) (see Steffen and Fothergill 2009), children also share a similar impulse and may too be frustrated if they are not able to find an outlet to help. It is thus crucially important that emergency managers and others who respond to crisis anticipate that children may want to help, and work to make space for the range of helping behaviors that children may wish to engage in or contribute to after disaster.

Although Katrina still stands as a distinctly devastating event in our national history, we are living in an era of more frequent and intense disasters. With the increased number of these events, it is all the more likely that this and future generations of children will continue to be engaged in pre- and post-disaster helping behaviors. Accordingly, we call for more nuanced analyses of how cultural, social, political, and technological practices and values within communities and broader societies influence children's participation in disaster risk reduction and climate change adaptation strategies as well as in disaster response and recovery. How do these different structures encourage or constrain their voices, actions, and involvement at local, regional, and national levels? How might our traditional means of data collection, reporting, and analysis also bias our understanding of children's responses to crisis? Anderson (2005) previously observed that children are often excluded from these very conversations about hazards and disasters (and other issues of social importance) because they cannot vote and are rarely included in decision-making processes. Similarly, children are often overlooked in terms of their contributions to civil society or not trusted as agentic thinkers, perhaps rendering them as invisible agents in bottom-up responses to crisis.

Moreover, the complexity of children's experiences, actions, and group characteristics require further investigation. Although Katrina was perhaps the most obviously racialized disaster of modern history (Dyson 2006), the news media rarely identified the race of the children who were helping or the race of those who they were working to help. Similarly, we know little about the motivations for the children's helping behaviors, nor whether those behaviors in the immediate aftermath of the storm translated into longer-term personal or social transformations.

Although gaps in knowledge persist, it is clear that there has been movement for a more grassroots, inclusive, child-centered disaster risk reduction agenda in recent years, such as the efforts witnessed at the Child and Youth Forum of the Third United Nations World Conference on Disaster Risk Reduction in Sendai, Japan (Cumiskey et al. 2015). At that conference, young people from around the world made their desire to become critical players in disaster risk reduction apparent. How much systemic change will result from that action is still an open question. What is clear, however, is that both disaster-affected and non-disaster-affected children can contribute in meaningful ways to reducing risk and supporting those who have lived through crisis. This chapter has shown that non-disaster affected children raised their hands and were ready to help after Katrina, and their contributions were substantial. Recognizing these contributions represents an important step toward further legitimizing the space they deserve to hold in civic society and democratizing discourses around disasters.

Notes

1. Oronde is a pseudonym. He was a participant in a study focused on children's long-term recovery in the aftermath of Hurricane Katrina (see Fothergill and Peek 2015).
2. For more information, visit http://therethinkers.org/.
3. For more information on the special issue, visit https://www.jstor.org/stable/10.7721/chilyoutenvi.18.issue-1.
4. The larger dataset includes 205 news stories regarding children's helping behaviors in response to some of the costliest and deadliest disasters of the early twenty-first century, including the 9/11 terrorist attacks, 2004 Hurricane Charley, 2004 Hurricane Ivan, 2004 Hurricane Wilma, 2004 Indian Ocean Earthquake and Tsunami, 2005 Hurricane Katrina, 2005 Hurricane Rita, 2008 Hurricane Ike, 2010 Haiti Earthquake, 2010 British Petroleum (BP) Oil Spill, 2011 Japan Earthquake and Tsunami, 2011 Joplin Tornado, and 2012 Superstorm Sandy. We focus specifically on Hurricane Katrina in this chapter as the bulk of the media coverage (108 articles, or nearly 53 percent of all the articles that we found) concentrated on that disaster. Given space constraints with this chapter, we plan to complete cross-disaster and cross-national analyses of the additional media coverage in future work.

References

Abramson, D., K. Brooks, and L. Peek. 2014. The Science and Practice of Resilience Interventions for Children Exposed to Disasters. In *Preparedness, Response, and Recovery Considerations for Children and Families: Workshop Summary*, ed. T. Wizemann, M. Reeve, and B.M. Altevogt, 177–202. Washington, DC: The National Academies Press.

Anderson, W.A. 2005. Bringing Children into Focus on the Social Science Disaster Research Agenda. *International Journal of Mass Emergencies and Disasters* 23 (3): 159–175.

Averill, J. 2005. Bangor High Students Organize Rock for Relief. *Bangor Daily News*, September 21, B4.

Back, E., C. Cameron, and T. Tanner. 2009. *Children and Disaster Risk Reduction: Taking Stock and Moving Forward*. UNICEF Research Report: Children in a Changing Climate Research. https://www.preventionweb.net/files/15093_1 2085ChildLedDRRTakingStock1.pdf.

Bartlett, S. 2008. After the Tsunami in Cooks Nagar: The Challenges of Participatory Rebuilding. *Children, Youth and Environments* 18 (1): 470–484.

Cho, H. 2005. State's Students Give for Katrina. *The Baltimore Sun*, October 18, n.p.

Cumiskey, L., T. Hoang, S. Suzuki, C. Pettigrew, and M.M. Herrgård. 2015. Youth Participation at the Third UN World Conference on Disaster Risk Reduction. *International Journal of Disaster Risk Science* 6 (2): 150–163.

DeFour, M. 2011. Youth Share Service Trip to New Orleans. *Wisconsin State Journal*, May 22, C1.

Dyson, M.E. 2006. *Come Hell or High Water: Hurricane Katrina and the Color of Disaster*. New York: Basic Civitas.

Fletcher, S., R.S. Cox, L. Scannell, C. Heykoop, J. Tobin-Gurley, and L. Peek. 2016. Youth Creating Disaster Recovery and Resilience: A Multi-Site Arts-Based Youth Engagement Project. *Children, Youth and Environments* 26 (1): 148–163.

Florida Times Union. 2005. Backpacks for Katrina Victims. *The Florida Times Union*, September 28, M8.

Fothergill, A., and L. Peek. 2015. *Children of Katrina*. Austin: University of Texas Press.

Frazier, L. 2007. 9-Year-Old Philanthropist Maintains Can-Do Attitude. *The Tampa Tribune*, July 21, 4.

Haynes, K., and T.M. Tanner. 2015. Empowering Young People and Strengthening Resilience: Youth-centred Participatory Video as a Tool for Climate Change Adaptation and Disaster Risk Reduction. *Children's Geographies* 13 (3): 357–371.

Hussey, M. 2005. Boxes for Evacuees a Lesson in Giving. *The Tampa Tribune*, October 8, 13.

Javid-Yazdi, M. 2007. Students Connect with Katrina Victims. *The Orange County Register*, February 8, 1.

Jeffrey, C. 2011. Youth and Development. *European Journal of Development Research* 23 (5): 792–796.

Johnson, M. L. 2005. Sending Something South: St. Augustine Youngsters Try to Lift Spirits of Hurricane Victims. *South Bend Tribune*, December 1, n.p.

Kid4Kid 2017. Our founder. *Kid4Kid*, n.p. http://www.kid4kid.com/our-founder/.

Kids to the Rescue. 2017. About Kids to the Rescue. *Kids to the Rescue*, n.p. http://www.kidstotherescue.org/about_kttr.htm.

Kilbride, K. 2005. Moran Students Contribute to Relief: Items for More than 200 Health Kits Gathered. *South Bend Tribune*, September 22, n.p.

Livingstone, D. 2006. Kids Help Hometown and One Hit by Storm. *Portland Press Herald*, August 3, F2.

Lopez, Y., J. Hayden, K. Cologon, and F. Hadley. 2012. Child Participation and Disaster Risk Reduction. *International Journal of Early Years Education* 20 (3): 300–308.

Marchezini, V., and R. Trajber. 2017. Youth-based Learning in Disaster Risk Reduction Education. In *Responses to Disasters and Climate Change: Understanding Vulnerability and Fostering Resilience*, ed. M. Companion and M.S. Chaiken, 27–36. Boca Raton, FL: CRC Press.

Martin, M.L. 2010. Child Participation in Disaster Risk Reduction: The Case of Flood-affected Children in Bangladesh. *Third World Quarterly* 31 (8): 1357–1375.

Mitchell, T., K. Haynes, N. Hall, W. Choong, and K. Oven. 2008. The Role of Children and Youth in Communicating Disaster Risk. *Children, Youth and Environments* 18 (1): 254–279.

Mitchell, T., T. Tanner, and K. Haynes. 2009. *Children as Agents of Change for DRR: Lessons from El Salvador and Philippines*. Children in a Changing Climate Research Working Paper No. 1. http://www.undpcc.org/undpcc/files/docs/publications/CCC_Working%20Paper_Final1_Screen.pdf.

Moore, K. 2006. Students Learn How to Respond to Those in Need. *Contra Costa Times*, February 3, F4.

Peek, L. 2008. Children and Disasters: Understanding Vulnerability, Developing Capacities, and Promoting Resilience—An Introduction. *Children, Youth and Environments* 18 (1): 1–29.

Peek, L., and K. Richardson. 2010. In Their Own Words: Displaced Children's Educational Recovery Needs after Hurricane Katrina. *Disaster Medicine and Public Health Preparedness* 4 (3): S63–S70.

Peek, L., J. Tobin, R. Cox, S. Leila, S. Fletcher, and C. Heykoop. 2016. Engaging Youth in Post-disaster Research: Lessons Learned from a Creative Methods Approach. *Gateways: International Journal of Community Research and Engagement* 9 (1): 89–112.

Peek, L., D. Abramson, R. Cox, A. Fothergill, and J. Tobin. 2018. Children and Disasters. In *Handbook of Disaster Research*, ed. H. Rodriguez, W. Donner, and J.E. Trainor, 2nd ed., 243–262. New York: Springer.

Phillips, B.D. 2009. *Disaster Recovery*. Boca Raton, FL: CRC Press.

Pugh, A.J. 2014. The Theoretical Costs of Ignoring Childhood: Rethinking Independence, Insecurity, and Inequality. *Theory and Society* 43 (1): 71–89.

Ramirez, E. 2005. Katrina Teaches Lesson in Empathy. *St. Petersburg Times*, October 15, 1.

RandomKid. 2010. Our Story. *RandomKid*. http://www.randomkid.org/content/60/our-story.html.

Rivlin, G. 2015. *Katrina: After the Flood*. New York: Simon and Schuster.

Sloan, D. 2005. 'She Likes Doing Things for People': Henrico Girl's Bracelet Sales Raise Nearly $300 for Victims of Katrina. *Richmond Times-Dispatch*, September 23, A8.

Smith, J. 2006. Rebuilding with Legos. *Pittsfield Berkshire Eagle*, September 18, 43.

Steffen, S.L., and A. Fothergill. 2009. 9/11 Volunteerism: A Pathway to Personal Healing and Community Engagement. *Social Science Journal* 46 (1): 29–46.

Storr, V.H., S. Haeffele-Balch, and L.E. Grube. 2015. *Community Revival in the Wake of Disaster: Lessons in Local Entrepreneurship*. New York: Palgrave Macmillan.

Tanner, T. 2010. Shifting the Narrative: Child-led Responses to Climate Change and Disasters in El Salvador and the Philippines. *Children & Society* 24 (4): 339–351.

Towers, B., K. Haynes, F. Sewell, H. Bailie, and D. Cross. 2014. Child-centred Disaster Risk Reduction in Australia: Progress, Gaps and Opportunities. *Australian Journal of Emergency Management* 29 (1): 31–38.

Vanden Brook, T. 2005. Many Kids Lending a Hand by Opening Lemonade Stands. *USA Today*, September 6, n.p.

Weingarten, A. 2007. Church's Youth Treat Teenagers from New Orleans to Vacation. *Sarasota Herald-Tribune*, January 4, BM5.

Wiggins, O. 2007. Beltsville Girl's Gift to 'Katrina Kids:' Raising Money for Others, One Paper Fan at a Time. *Washington Post*, December 20, PG01.

7

Bottom-Up State-Building

Jennifer Murtazashvili and Ilia Murtazashvili

7.1 Introduction

The US has invested tremendous resources over the past several decades in an effort to fix fragile states. These state-building efforts in places such as Afghanistan, Iraq, and Somalia often proceed in top-down fashion, with emphasis on constructing a national government capable of implementing public policies. This perspective is rooted in Weberian conceptions of a rational-legal state, which is characterized mainly by meritorious bureaucracy (Weber 1978). Working from the Weberian tradition, Fukuyama (2013) conceptualizes of the quality of governance as the

We thank Virgil Henry Storr and Stefanie Haeffele, and the participants in the Hayek Program, Scholars Responding to Crisis Symposium at the Mercatus Center at George Mason University, for exceptionally useful comments.

J. Murtazashvili (✉) • I. Murtazashvili
Graduate School of Public and International Affairs, University of Pittsburgh, Pittsburgh, PA, USA
e-mail: jmurtaz@pitt.edu; ilia.murtazashvili@pitt.edu

© The Author(s) 2020
S. Haeffele, V. H. Storr (eds.), *Bottom-up Responses to Crisis*, Mercatus Studies in Political and Social Economy, https://doi.org/10.1007/978-3-030-39312-0_7

capacity and autonomy of the national government to implement policies. According to this line of thought, successful crisis response depends on the quality of the national government, defined in terms of its capacity and autonomy.

We question the top-down approach to state-building. Our alternative approach is based on the bottom-up approach to crisis response and recovery. The bottom-up approach to crisis response and recovery is pluralistic, using insights from Austrian economics, public choice, and the Bloomington School of institutional analysis to address how well a society responds to crises arising from nature or from human behavior. Although these schools of thought are often considered separately, they provide complementary insight into the political, economic, and social/cultural dimensions of recovery from crises (Boettke et al. 2007; Sobel and Leeson 2006, 2007).

To date, the bottom-up approach to crisis has mainly been used to illustrate recovery from natural disasters in the US, especially devastating hurricanes. These studies find that the federal and state governments contribute to slower, costlier, and less effective responses to natural disasters than community responses coordinated through market and civil society institutions (Chamlee-Wright and Storr 2009a, b; Storr et al. 2017). Rather than government intervention, community response and recovery was more effective when markets were allowed to allocate resources in response to changes in relative prices (e.g., Horwitz 2009), as well as when communities were more tightly knit (e.g., Chamlee-Wright and Storr 2011). These perspectives do not deny a role for the government, but they clarify that its most important function is to provide law and order, including policing crime against businesses, and protecting private property.

Of course, there is an important difference in fragile states. In such contexts, formal political and economic institutions are often incoherent (Bromley and Anderson 2012). Does this incoherence of formal institutions require a top-down response to the crisis of state fragility?

We clarify why the bottom-up approach is still relevant to post-conflict reconstruction of fragile states. Like the accounts of response to natural disasters, the political economy of post-conflict reconstruction has a political, economic, and social dimension. Our perspective can be called bottom-up state-building. Its defining features include efforts to establish more effective political institutions at the local level, rather than by a focus on national institutions and national elections; economic reforms, especially those which strengthen self-governing property institutions; and working with customary and tribal institutions during the reconstruction process.

We use lessons from Afghanistan to illustrate the political economy of post-conflict reconstruction. We begin by showing how government contributed to the collapse of the Afghan state. After 2001, the international community, working with the Afghan government, attempted to create a more powerful state. Despite these investments, government authorities remained an unreliable option for most Afghans. Instead, customary institutions provided a far more important and stable source of governance in the context of state weakness. Unfortunately, the international community often worked to eschew these vital organizations, either ignoring them or seeking to work around them. As the Afghan state struggled to gain legitimacy during the 15 years after 2001, customary authorities adapted and remained the lifeline of governance for most Afghans, especially those in rural areas. Bottom-up state-building appears more important than ever to improve prospects for political order and economic development in Afghanistan.

7.2   Political, Economic, and Social Dimensions of State-Building

Much of the literature on crisis considers society's response to natural disasters. Some of the challenges in this domain are similar to those facing a community after a natural disaster, such as shortages. Yet the typical fragile state also confronts a legacy of extractive political institutions, inability of the government to perform basic administrative tasks (such as policing, and corrupt courts), and of course, a violent legacy. Formal economic institutions are often poorly designed or weak. War and conflict can also undermine social and cultural institutions, as does a legacy of migration or repopulation campaigns designed to achieve bureaucratic priorities. They are crises that involve the fickleness of nature, but they also involve the folly of man.

State-building efforts face political constraints. Prior to state collapse, political institutions are typically extractive, which is one of the reasons that state collapse in some cases may make society better off. According to Leeson (2007), a predatory state can be worse than no state, as long as self-governance works well. Yet there is also a powerful and important justification for state-building. According to the economic theory of the state, government emerges in order to more efficiently provide public goods, such as security and protection of property (North and Thomas 1973; North 1981; Barzel 2002). These theories also recognize the importance of constraints on the government in order for rulers to establish institutions that promote economic development (North and Weingast 1989).[1] Thus, the emergence of a government, provided Leviathan is constrained, promises to facilitate long-run economic development and political order, such as by providing an institutional framework to regulate a market economy.

There are several challenges to implementing this vision of a limited government that encourages market exchange in post-conflict settings. Efforts to transplant democratic institutions may not fit with existing norms and therefore result in conflict (Coyne 2008). Another challenge is that the government may not be able to commit credibly to economic reforms (Coyne and Boettke 2009). Foreign aid can undermine political institutions (Dutta et al. 2013). Development assistance can also result in vicious cycles of aid, dependence, and reinforcement of preexisting, inefficient institutions (Murtazashvili 2016a).

There is also an economic dimension to post-conflict reconstruction. Ultimately, political order depends on economic development. Without economic development, the government will be unable to provide public goods (Levi 1988). The state is not the only source of public goods, which are often provided privately, including national defense, courts, and policing (Clark and Powell 2019). Rather, it means that to the extent the government is able to provide public goods, it depends on economic development.

What economic institutions promote economic development? The usual economic response is to create private property rights to promote economic growth and development (Acemoglu and Johnson 2005). The reason is because private property rights create incentives for production, rather than predation. Private property, along with entrepreneurs, also provides incentives for innovation in the economy (Kirzner 1978).[2]

Private property institutions are often provided by the state as a public good (Olson 1993; North 1981). More generally, capitalism requires a legal framework to thrive (Hodgson 2015; Deakin et al. 2017). However, post-conflict states often lack property rights or coherent economic institutions more generally.

The political and economic dimensions of reform are also interrelated in at least two ways. One is that establishing the "right" economic institutions depends on the structure of political institutions. Polycentric institutions can improve the chances that economic institutions produce better outcomes. Another is that to implement economic reforms, the state requires at least some bureaucratic competence. Such bureaucratic competence, including quality legal institutions, increases the ability to "transplant" institutions to a new context, including private property rights (Berkowitz et al. 2001, 2003; Boettke et al. 2008). However, many contexts lack effective legal institutions, which can result in challenges implementing institutional reforms, such as legal property rights (Blattman et al. 2014).

Finally, reconstruction efforts have a social/cultural dimension. In economics, anarchy is the absence of state control of behavior (Leeson 2006). Anarchy sometimes leads to conflict, but in many instances, self-governance works well (Leeson 2014). According to these studies, tightly knit communities often find ways to organize their affairs when the government's rules are inefficient (Skarbek 2011, 2014). When the club is more tightly knit, it is more likely to provide public goods (Chamlee-Wright and Storr 2009a). Hence, social capital influences disaster response (Chamlee-Wright and Storr 2011).

Post-conflict states are often described as ungoverned. The economics of anarchy suggests that this thinking is misguided. Private governance often works better than the state (Stringham 2015). This is especially the case in weak and fragile states, where people are often able to rely on communities because the state is unreliable, corrupt, or weak (Scott 1999).

Organizations may also be a source of economic institutions, such as property rights. In some contexts, entrepreneurs may provide property protection for a profit. These protective entrepreneurs can be a source of economic development (Leeson and Boettke 2009). Criminal organizations, such as a mafia or gang, can also be a source of governance, especially when formal government rules are inefficient (Piano 2017; Skarbek 2014; Leeson and Rogers 2012).

This framework suggests that the success of reconstruction efforts will depend on each of these three dimensions. The political dimension suggests the key is not to establish a strong national government, but one that is a limited government. It is also necessary to establish effective local institutions that encourage political participation, especially in states where the government has typically been centralized. The economic challenge is to establish more effective economic institutions, which may involve formalization of spontaneously arising property institutions. The social dimension will typically involve identification of local partners in reconstruction whose authority derives from custom or from tribal ties.

We illustrate this framework by considering state-building efforts in Afghanistan, where the expensive reconstruction effort failed to deliver on its promise of political order and economic development. One plausible explanation is new institutions reflect weakness on the political and economic dimensions, as well as lack of appreciation for self-governance.

7.3   The Political Economy of the Collapse of the Afghan State

Afghanistan has been mired in conflict for the last several decades. The country descended into a civil war shortly after the People's Democratic Party of Afghanistan (PDPA), its main communist party, seized power in April 1978. After the communist government collapsed in 1992, factions fought for control. By 1996, the Taliban government controlled much of the country. In 2001, the US and Afghan Northern Alliance allies removed the Taliban from power. War resulted in the collapse of the state (though not completely, as centralized bureaucratic institutions remained in place and still exist after a decade and a half of state-building). Since that time, the country has been the site of a massive state-building effort. There have been several rounds of national elections since then, but economic stability is questionable, and the country has remained mired in violence.

To see the importance of the political dimension in post-conflict reconstruction, it is useful to consider the role of government policy in state failure. Historically, rulers have used state ownership of land and repopulation to consolidate political power. Rather than consolidate authority and provide private property protection to encourage production, Afghan rulers have preferred weakening private property to exert control (Murtazashvili and Murtazashvili 2016d). During the late nineteenth century, Abdur Rahman, who ruled with an iron fist from 1880 to 1901, used land repopulation as a way to weaken ethnic groups and to establish loyalty to the Afghan government. He believed that by tearing people from their traditional homelands, they would be more dependent on the Afghan state for support in their new lands, and therefore more loyal to him. The end result, in his view, was that they would be less likely to revolt having been purged from the ties that bound them to their traditional lands. Abdur Rahman also believed that if he kept his defeated adversaries poor that they would never revolt or challenge his authority again (Barfield 2010). One way he tried to ensure their quiescence was to prohibit railroads. He believed that without railroads, foreign armies would have a more challenging time moving around the country, but it would also ensure that Afghanistan would be less attractive to colonial powers because it would remain a poor country.

Even as there was some progress in establishing private property in the twentieth century, the governments in the 1930s through 1960s used land policies to move people around for political purposes (Murtazashvili and Murtazashvili 2016b). Like their predecessor Abdur Rahman, these governments believed that land repopulation could promote economic development, although when these groups were resettled, they were often excluded from legal protection or recognition in their new homes

(Malkasian 2013). Rather than establish private property institutions, the government relied more on subsidies, with the vast majority of government revenue coming from foreign aid (Barfield 2010; Rubin 2002). This was a time of political stability—it was Afghanistan's long peace—but there was almost no economic development and the state was notional in the sense it did not have the revenue to sustain its functioning without foreign assistance.

In the 1950s, Afghanistan's main communist party, the PDPA, emerged. In April 1978, the Khalq, the radical faction of the PDPA, seized power in a palace coup against Mohammed Daud, the first person to take the title of president of Afghanistan (previous rulers were called amirs or khans). Although Daud was left-leaning, the Khalq believed that he was too timid in his economic policies, preferring instead a vanguard-style revolution to break what they perceived as conditions of feudalism in the country.

The Khalq policies demonstrated a profound misunderstanding of customary institutions. Rather than feudalism, many Afghans owned land privately, although they did not have legal title. Rural Afghans opposed land redistribution because of strong norms of private ownership (Edwards 2002). The communist government also misunderstood the role of tribal khans, who were not feudal institutions but better described as self-financed public servants providing public goods locally (Anderson 1978).

The Afghan communist revolution contributed to decades of conflict and violence, including to the rise of the Taliban, which emerged as an anti-Soviet insurgency before it was driven to Pakistan where it would lie in wait until the early 1990s. After the PDPA government fell in 1992, rival alliances waged bitter campaigns. During this time, the Taliban returned from Pakistan. By 1996, the Taliban controlled much of the country, although Northern Alliance forces never fully conceded. The Taliban reforms included returning stolen lands. However, the Taliban was not especially concerned with economic development. They promoted the poppy trade but imposed harsh taxes on farmers and traders (Rashid 2010). Economic development declined to even lower levels than during the long peace.

In 2001, the US military and Afghan Northern Alliance allies, working in many cases side by side with US Special Forces, removed the Taliban from power. Since then, there has been trillions spent to construct a more competent state. Despite these investments, state-building has not been effective. The reasons can be divided into political, economic, and social dimensions.

7.4 Why State-Building Failed to Deliver on its Promise

7.4.1 The Political Dimension

One challenge to effective state-building is that the Afghan state remains highly centralized, at least on paper, even though it has long been a de facto federation (Murtazashvili 2014). The legacy of rulers from Abdur Rahman to the communist governments was centralization of formal political authority. Political centralization is a persistent source of conflict in a society with robust informal institutions that tie people together in their communities. Despite its drawbacks, the post-2001 Afghan state remained extremely centralized. All budget and appointment authority for local officials came from Kabul. Village elections were promised in the 2001 constitution, but have not yet been held (Jochem et al. 2016). There have been national elections, but each round has been characterized by substantial allegations of corruption (Coburn and Larson 2014; Jochem et al. forthcoming).

One of the consequences of these developments is that parchment political institutions do not fit well with preexisting institutions. Government institutions still do not account adequately for local power structures. Customary governance, which is often effective in providing public goods, including dispute resolution, at the local level, has no formal authority in the government. There have been national elections, but formal democracy at the village level has yet to be seen. The de facto polycentric structure is continually undermined by formal institutional rules that vest authority in the central government.

Foreign aid exacerbates the political problem. The preexisting political institutions—those which existed prior to decades of civil war—were poorly designed, as they too were a poor fit with existing institutions in the country. The vestiges of these institutions also remained, and working through them provided a path of least resistance as foreign aid began to flow into the country (Murtazashvili 2016a). Such reliance is typical bureaucratic rationality. It also contributes to vicious cycles of aid, dependence, and absence of needed political reform.

7.4.2   The Economic Dimension

The quality of formal economic institutions in Afghanistan remains unable to promote sustained growth. Prior to 1978, there was some development of legal private property. However, the revolution of 1978 introduced additional uncertainty to the property situation. One source of uncertainty was a fear of land expropriation, but another was that the revolution weakened the state's ability to administer legal property relations. The violence that accompanied the revolution also cut short the cadastral survey that had been planned. Today, the country has still not completed a cadastral survey (Alden Wily 2013). Very few people have legal titles in rural areas, in part because the government still has very limited ability to record land ownership.

There have been some efforts to improve private property. However, legal titling projects have not worked well (Deschamps and Roe 2009; Gaston and Dang 2015). There remain challenges of implementing land reform, even in places like Kabul and Kandahar where the government has had a stronger presence (AREU 2017). After a decade and a half of state-building, there remained very little progress in establishing formal economic institutions, even those that simply recognize de facto ownership rights to land.

7.4.3   The Social/Cultural Dimension

The social/cultural dimension may be the greatest cause for optimism with regard to Afghan state-building. The Afghanistan state was founded through a customary and decentralized procedure (Barfield 2010). In

1747, tribal and customary leaders came together to choose military general Ahmad Shah as the first king in a Loya Jirga, or national assembly. He was given part of the declining Afsharid empire of Nadir Shah. It was a nomadic empire that subsisted on conquest. There was not much to this state. Blood relatives held onto fiefdoms. They frequently launched revolts against the political center. There was some centralization in the mid-nineteenth century, but the country remained organized around customary institutions (Noelle 1997). There was no real standing army. Tribal conscripts, or lashkhars, played a critical role in pushing back the British during the two Anglo-Afghan wars from 1839–1842 and 1878–1880 (Johnson 2012).

Despite its significance in Afghan affairs, rulers in Afghanistan have more generally tried to weaken the authority of customary governance. Abdur Rahman tried to eliminate it during several violent campaigns, which he waged against any groups that opposed his rule. His target was the largely self-governing communities, which he viewed as a source of weakness.

Customary governance persisted even though Abdur Rahman was able to defeat most of his rivals. Abdur Rahman's grandson, Amanullah (r. 1919–1929), was a social and economic reformer who recognized that development required openness and private property. But his reforms came in conflict with a tribal society, and he was ousted by a Tajik warrior-peasant after a short civil war (Poullada 1973). Although Amanullah was a reformer, like his grandfather, he had little patience for customary governance. Indeed, he declared that the only legal property was that which is recognized by the state, which had the effect of ensuring that customary property ownership and customary dispute resolution had no legal authority.

The communist government also waged a campaign against customary and tribal institutions. For reasons noted earlier, the communist government believed that informal institutions were a source of economic underdevelopment. They had little patience for customary governance. Rather than work with them, the communists attempted to co-opt customary leaders or replace them with their own people.

One of the surprising features of the current context is the persistent yet adaptive nature of customary governance. Murtazashvili (2016b) collected ethnographic field data in over thirty villages to understand sources of order in communities and found that customary authority remained quite resilient during the past forty years, but was transformed because of conflict.

In general, customary organizations at the community level have a structure that transcends ethnic group. In most communities, customary governance consists of three main organizations: village representatives (such as maliks, arbabs, qaryadars, etc.), deliberative councils (shrua/jirga), and religious figures (mullahs). Maliks are village leaders but are typically first among equals rather than chiefs. They serve as administrators, sometimes obtaining a stamp from local governors but have no formal legal authority. The shura is a deliberative council that, in theory, includes the participation of all households in the community through male representatives. Mullahs are village-based religious authorities.

The findings from fieldwork differed dramatically from what one might expect. Customary authority even after decades of conflict remain an important source of public goods provision and governance in an environment in which the state has questionable authority, legitimacy, and capacity.

An important example is property institutions. In Afghanistan, customary land relations are a source of property security, more than the state (Murtazashvili and Murtazashvili 2016c). In such contexts, legal titling makes little sense because self-governance works well (Murtazashvili and Murtazashvili 2015). Yet the international community has recognized that there is an alternative between doing nothing and legal titling. The most successful land policies that have been implemented are community-based ones that eschew a role for the state (Murtazashvili and Murtazashvili 2016a). These community-based policies recognize a role for self-governance but target aid to technologies that better record land ownership at the community level, without inviting an untrusted state into community land relations.

One of the few areas of decentralized aid delivery that truly works with communities is in land registration. Theses community-based projects do not aspire to legal recognition. Indeed, legal titling has not worked well, but the community-based projects have improved household land-tenure security.

There have been other local development programs, although some have come into conflict with preexisting institutions. The National Solidarity Program is one of the largest development projects implemented in the country. Its purpose is to provide for local government in the countryside, which is based on the presumption that war destabilized customary decision-making structures. The program provided funding to villages and established village councils to decide how to distribute aid funds. Evaluations found that the NSP undermined the quality of governance in the communities where it has been implemented (Beath et al. 2015). It is also clear that the premise of the program—the breakdown of customary governance—was not a reality in most communities. Rather, the project provided an additional layer of local governance. This additional layer of governance created competition for authority in communities that undermined governance outcomes in rural areas at a time when public authority remained very fragile (Murtazashvili 2016b).

7.5 Conclusion

A bottom-up approach to state-building holds promise in explaining why state-building fails to deliver on its promise. The first feature of decentralized state-building is recognizing that centralized political institutions may often come into conflict with de facto systems of polycentric governance. These centralized political institutions are often strengthened by foreign assistance. Another challenge is that elections are prioritized over economic reform. A third challenge is that although customary governance is often effective, it is often viewed as an obstacle to development. Hence, opportunities for fruitful collaboration are often lost.

These perspectives provide insight into the failure of post-conflict reconstruction in Afghanistan. Rather than a solution, the current structure of the Afghan government is an obstacle to political stability, as it remains highly centralized even though it is de facto polycentric, which creates conflict between communities and government. State-building has emphasized establishing democracy over reform of economic institutions. There have been several rounds of national elections, but it is challenging to discern lasting reform of economic institutions.

The economic literature on anarchy also anticipates the importance of self-governance in Afghanistan. Even though the Afghan state has attempted to eliminate customary and tribal governance, it remains an important option for many Afghans who cannot rely on the state. Yet bureaucratic proclivities of the state-building bureaucracy do not always recognize a role for self-governance. The international community in many instances eschews customary governance. There remains no formal representation of customary governance in the government, no clear recognition of customary adjudication by courts, no legal recognition of customary deeds in the legal property regime, and so on. Thus, although self-governance remains an option, it is important to avoid seeing like a foreign aid NGO, which often works through inefficient government institutions or building new organizations that mimic their own goals, values, and structures, rather than with communities.

There are lessons for post-conflict reconstruction beyond the case at hand. Elections do not substitute for improvements in public administration. The latter is perhaps more essential to improving provision of public goods and services. Nor are elections a substitute for economic reform. These economic reforms should also avoid turning into development planning since in many contexts, spontaneously arising institutions can generate growth. The challenge of economic reform is to identify what reforms are effective and those that are not, rather than imposing new institutions from the top down. Finally, it is essential that these efforts consider carefully the appropriate role for communities in the process of post-conflict reconstruction. Self-governance and social capital are often some of the most valuable assets in post-conflict settings.

Notes

1. Salter (2015) explains that ownership may also contribute to the extent to which political institutions are constrained.
2. Though it should be noted that private property rights create monopoly privileges than under certain conditions can be a source of inefficiency (Posner and Weyl 2017), and in some instances, there is important innovation without private property (Moser 2013).

References

Acemoglu, D., and S. Johnson. 2005. Unbundling Institutions. *Journal of Political Economy* 113 (5): 949–995.

Alden Wily, L. 2013. *Land, People, and the State in Afghanistan*. Kabul, Afghanistan: Afghanistan Research and Evaluation Unit (AREU).

Anderson, J. 1978. There Are No Khāns Anymore: Economic Development and Social Change in Tribal Afghanistan. *Middle East Journal* 32 (2): 167–183.

AREU. 2017. *Land Governance Assessment Framework (LGAF) – Afghanistan*. Kabul, Afghanistan: Afghanistan Research and Evaluation Unit (AREU).

Barfield, T.J. 2010. *Afghanistan: A Cultural and Political History*. Princeton: Princeton University Press.

Barzel, Y.A. 2002. *Theory of the State: Economic Rights, Legal Rights, and the Scope of the State*. New York: Cambridge University Press.

Beath, A., F. Christia, and R. Enikolopov. 2015. The National Solidarity Programme: Assessing the Effects of Community-Driven Development in Afghanistan. *International Peacekeeping* 22 (4): 302–320.

Berkowitz, D., K. Pistor, and J.-F. Richard. 2001. Economic Development, Legality, and the Transplant Effect. *European Economic Review* 47 (1): 165–195.

———. 2003. The Transplant Effect. *American Journal of Comparative Law* 51 (1): 163.

Blattman, C., A. Hartman, and R. Blair. 2014. How to Promote Order and Property Rights under Weak Rule of Law? An Experiment in Changing Dispute Resolution Behavior through Community Education. *American Political Science Review* 108 (1): 100–120.

Boettke, P.J., E. Chamlee-Wright, P. Gordon, S. Ikeda, Pe.T. Leeson, and R. Sobel. 2007. The Political, Economic, and Social Aspects of Katrina. *Southern Economic Journal* 74 (2): 363–376.

Boettke, P.J., C.J. Coyne, and P.T. Leeson. 2008. Institutional Stickiness and the New Development Economics. *American Journal of Economics and Sociology* 67 (2): 331–358.

Bromley, D.W., and G. Anderson. 2012. *Vulnerable People, Vulnerable States: Redefining the Development Challenge*. New York: Routledge.

Chamlee-Wright, E., and V.H. Storr. 2009a. Club Goods and Post-Disaster Community Return. *Rationality and Society* 21 (4): 429–458.

———. 2009b. 'There's No Place like New Orleans:' Sense of Place and Community Recovery in the Ninth Ward after Hurricane Katrina. *Journal of Urban Affairs* 31 (5): 615–634.

———. 2011. Social Capital as Collective Narratives and Post-disaster Community Recovery. *The Sociological Review* 59 (2): 266–282.

Clark, J.R., and B. Powell. 2019. The 'Minimal' State Reconsidered: Governance on the Margin. *The Review of Austrian Economics* 32 (2): 119–130.

Coburn, N., and A. Larson. 2014. *Derailing Democracy in Afghanistan: Elections in an Unstable Political Landscape*. New York: Columbia University Press.

Coyne, C.J. 2008. *After War: The Political Economy of Exporting Democracy*. Stanford: Stanford University Press.

Coyne, C.J., and P.J. Boettke. 2009. The Problem of Credible Commitment in Reconstruction. *Journal of Institutional Economics* 5 (1): 1–23.

Deakin, S., D. Gindis, G.M. Hodgson, K. Huang, and K. Pistor. 2017. Legal Institutionalism: Capitalism and the Constitutive Role of Law. *Journal of Comparative Economics* 45 (1): 188–200.

Deschamps, C., and A. Roe. 2009. *Land Conflict in Afghanistan: Building Capacity to Address Vulnerability*. Kabul, Afghanistan: Afghanistan Research and Evaluation Unit (AREU).

Dutta, N., P.T. Leeson, and C.R. Williamson. 2013. The Amplification Effect: Foreign Aid's Impact on Political Institutions. *Kyklos* 66 (2): 208–228.

Edwards, D.B. 2002. *Before Taliban: Genealogies of the Afghan Jihad*. Berkeley: University of California Press.

Fukuyama, F. 2013. What Is Governance? *Governance* 26 (3): 347–368.

Gaston, E., and L. Dang. 2015. *Addressing Land Conflict in Afghanistan*. United States Institute for Peace Special Report 372.

Hodgson, G.M. 2015. *Conceptualizing Capitalism: Institutions, Evolution, Future*. Chicago: University of Chicago Press.

Horwitz, S. 2009. Wal-Mart to the Rescue: Private Enterprise's Response to Hurricane Katrina. *The Independent Review* 13 (4): 511–528.

Jochem, T., I. Murtazashvili, and J. Murtazashvili. 2016. Establishing Local Government in Fragile States: Experimental Evidence from Afghanistan. *World Development* 77 (1): 293–310.

———. forthcoming. Can the Design of Electoral Institutions Improve Perceptions of Democracy in Fragile States? *Journal of Global Security Studies*. https://doi.org/10.1093/jogss/ogz020.

Johnson, R. 2012. *The Afghan Way of War: How and Why They Fight*. New York: Oxford University Press.

Kirzner, I.M. 1978. *Competition and Entrepreneurship*. Chicago: University of Chicago Press.

Leeson, P.T. 2006. Efficient Anarchy. *Public Choice* 130 (1–2): 41–53.

———. 2007. Better Off Stateless: Somalia Before and After Government Collapse. *Journal of Comparative Economics* 35 (4): 689–710.

———. 2014. *Anarchy Unbound: Why Self-Governance Works Better than You Think*. New York: Cambridge University Press.

Leeson, P.T., and P.J. Boettke. 2009. Two-Tiered Entrepreneurship and Economic Development. *International Review of Law and Economics* 29 (3): 252–259.

Leeson, P.T., and D.B. Rogers. 2012. Organizing Crime. *Supreme Court Economic Review* 20 (1): 89–123.

Levi, M. 1988. *Of Rule and Revenue*. Berkeley: University of California Press.

Malkasian, C. 2013. *War Comes to Garmser: Thirty Years of Conflict on the Afghan Frontier*. New York: Oxford University Press.

Moser, P. 2013. Patents and Innovation: Evidence from Economic History. *The Journal of Economic Perspectives* 27 (1): 23–44.

Murtazashvili, J. 2014. Informal Federalism: Self-Governance and Power Sharing in Afghanistan. *Publius* 44 (2): 324–343.

———. 2016a. Afghanistan: A Vicious Cycle of State Failure. *Governance* 29 (2): 163–166.

———. 2016b. *Informal Order and the State in Afghanistan*. New York: Cambridge University Press.

Murtazashvili, I., and J. Murtazashvili. 2015. Anarchy, Self-Governance, and Legal Titling. *Public Choice* 162 (3–4): 287–305.

———. 2016a. Can Community-Based Land Adjudication and Registration Improve Household Land Tenure Security? Evidence from Afghanistan. *Land Use Policy* 55: 230–239.

———. 2016b. Does the Sequence of Land Reform and Political Reform Matter? Evidence from State-Building in Afghanistan. *Conflict, Security & Development* 16 (2): 145–172.

———. 2016c. The Origins of Property Rights: States or Customary Organizations? *Journal of Institutional Economics* 12 (1): 105–128.

———. 2016d. When Does the Emergence of a Stationary Bandit Lead to Property Insecurity? *Rationality and Society* 28 (3): 335–360.

Noelle, C. 1997. *State and Tribe in Nineteenth-Century Afghanistan: The Reign of Amir Dost Muhammad Khan, 1826–1863*. New York: Routledge.

North, D.C. 1981. *Structure and Change in Economic History*. New York: W. W. Norton & Company.

North, D.C., and R.P. Thomas. 1973. *The Rise of the Western World: A New Economic History*. New York: Cambridge University Press.

North, D.C., and B.R. Weingast. 1989. Constitutions and Commitment: The Evolution of Institutions Governing Public Choice in Seventeenth-Century England. *The Journal of Economic History* 49 (4): 803–832.

Olson, M. 1993. Dictatorship, Democracy, and Development. *American Political Science Review* 87 (3): 567–576.

Piano, E.E. 2017. Free Riders: The Economics and Organization of Outlaw Motorcycle Gangs. *Public Choice* 171 (3–4): 283–301.

Posner, E.A., and E.G. Weyl. 2017. Property Is Only Another Name for Monopoly. *Journal of Legal Analysis* 9 (1): 51–123.

Poullada, L.B. 1973. *Reform and Rebellion in Afghanistan, 1919–1929; King Amanullah's Failure to Modernize a Tribal Society*. Ithaca, NY: Cornell University Press.

Rashid, A. 2010. *Taliban: Militant Islam, Oil and Fundamentalism in Central Asia*. New Haven, CT: Yale University Press.

Rubin, B.R. 2002. *The Fragmentation of Afghanistan: State Formation and Collapse in the International System*. New Haven, CT: Yale University Press.

Salter, A.W. 2015. Rights to the Realm: Reconsidering Western Political Development. *American Political Science Review* 109 (4): 725–734.

Scott, J.C. 1999. *Seeing Like a State: How Certain Schemes to Improve the Human Condition Have Failed*. New Haven, CT: Yale University Press.

Skarbek, D. 2011. Governance and Prison Gangs. *American Political Science Review* 105 (4): 702–716.

———. 2014. *The Social Order of the Underworld: How Prison Gangs Govern the American Penal System*. New York: Oxford University Press.

Sobel, R.S., and P.T. Leeson. 2006. Government's Response to Hurricane Katrina: A Public Choice Analysis. *Public Choice* 127 (1–2): 55–73.

———. 2007. The Use of Knowledge in Natural-Disaster Relief Management. *The Independent Review* 11 (4): 519–532.

Storr, V.H., L.E. Grube, and S. Haeffele-Balch. 2017. Polycentric Orders and Post-Disaster Recovery: A Case Study of One Orthodox Jewish Community Following Hurricane Sandy. *Journal of Institutional Economics* 13 (4): 875–897.

Stringham, E.P. 2015. *Private Governance: Creating Order in Economic and Social Life*. New York: Oxford University Press.

Weber, M. 1978. *Economy and Society: An Outline of Interpretive Sociology*. Berkeley: University of California Press.

8

Government Intervention Induced Structural Crises: Exploratory Notes on the Patterns of Evolution and Response

Paul Dragos Aligica and Thomas Savidge

8.1 Introduction

A "crisis" disrupts normal processes, challenging the functioning of existing social structures and institutional arrangements. At the same time, it creates opportunities for change. There is a vast literature examining various types of crises in different circumstances, as crises can be classified in a range starting from personal and psychological to natural disasters

The authors would like to express their gratitude to Stefanie Haeffele for her very constructive comments and for her feedback on previous versions of this chapter. We are fully responsible for all remaining errors of omission or commission.

P. D. Aligica (✉)
F. A. Hayek Program for Advanced Study in Philosophy, Politics, and Economics, Mercatus Center at George Mason University, Fairfax, VA, USA
e-mail: daligica@mercatus.gmu.edu

T. Savidge
George Mason University, Fairfax, VA, USA

© The Author(s) 2020
S. Haeffele, V. H. Storr (eds.), *Bottom-up Responses to Crisis*, Mercatus Studies in Political and Social Economy, https://doi.org/10.1007/978-3-030-39312-0_8

and to political and economic turmoil impacting large populations. Our focus will be on political and economic crises. More precisely, this chapter draws attention to the problem of government-induced structural economic crises and to the potential bottom-up responses to them. The chapter uses the crisis in Venezuela as both a case study and a vehicle for taking a closer look at the specific nature of such crises while emphasizing the role of social learning and entrepreneurship in these circumstances.

8.2   Crises Induced by Governments

A crisis involves an unstable situation where an important change occurs, usually with the possibility of an undesirable outcome. Thierry C. Pauchant and Ian I. Mitroff (1992, 15) define a crisis as "a disruption that physically affects a system as a whole and threatens its basic assumptions, its subjective sense of self, its existential core." Others have described crises as situations filled with uncertainty and urgency where the vital interests of society are threatened (Rosenthal et al. 2001). In addition, crises are described as sudden interruptions by unsettling events that create opportunities for major change (Baumgartner and Jones 1993). In the end, the variety of definitions points out to the diversity of crises—the diversity of their origins, modes of manifestation, and consequences. However, in almost all cases a political element is eventually present in one form or another.

During a crisis, social and political actors are expected to respond to the disruption to mitigate or avoid undesirable outcomes. In situations of political and economic turmoil, governments are often expected to act as the main coordinators of collective action (especially during the twentieth and twenty-first centuries in Western nations). These expectations and the processes they engender are currently the dominant ways of understanding the responses to crisis. Yet, it is important to note that state interventions may not always provide the mitigation or solution needed but, instead, may become a source for either exacerbation of the current crisis or for the creation of a new type of crisis. Government-induced crises, thus, may be "first order crises" (induced by an initial policy of the government) or "second order crises" (the result of an intervention of the government aiming to solve an already existing crisis). Obviously, there are also compounded crises where government interventions both create and exacerbate the crisis.

Robert Higgs' *Crisis and Leviathan* (1987) describes how a mix of factors, including real and perceived emergencies that led to the growth of American government over the twentieth century. For Higgs, both a political crisis (i.e. World War I) and an economic crisis (i.e. the Great Depression) provide an opportunity for government expansion, often beyond its constitutional limits. After the crisis recedes, government activities do retract but not completely back to the pre-crisis scope and size. Yet the crisis only explains a portion of the story. Higgs (1987) describes the dynamics set into motion, where the permanent increase in government is supported by a new ideology in addition to the entrenched bureaucrats and institutions. Higgs (1987, 73) elucidates how crises can breakdown ideological resistance to larger government in "creating opportunities for many people both within and without government to do well for themselves and hence to look more favorably on the new order."

Irrespective of how the growth of government is fueled, with the expansion of government, the possibility of a government-induced crisis increases. The more a government attempts to use the method of command-and-control, the more likely a government decision will have unintended consequences (see Mises 1990 [1920], 1981 [1922]); Hayek 1948; Lavoie 1985; Kirzner 1988). The command-and-control model of government assumes that a precise synoptic understanding of the situation is possible. But, as F. A. Hayek (1948) argued, central authorities often lack the ability to access and interpret the knowledge of *time* and *place*, of changes in information that are occurring in real time and which are best communicated through the price system. These failures of central planning are, in most cases, defining features of structural and long-term government-induced political and economic crises (Hayek 1948).

Significant and extreme instances of a government-induced crises can be found in the twentieth century socialist-communist regimes (see Grossman 1963, 1977; Bergson 1992; Boettke 2000, 2001; Bornstein 1989; Olson 1982). Numerous collectivization programs caused the death and starvation of millions under communist rule. Under Joseph Stalin's rule, the Soviet Union's forced collectivization to finance industrialization had disastrous effects on agricultural productivity. Soviet law mandated that no grain from a collective farm could be kept by its members until government mandated quotas were met. In 1932, Stalin raised Ukraine's grain procurement quotas that resulted in a famine that killed between six and seven million people the following year (US Commission on the Ukrainian Famine 1988). Further, the largest famine in human history occurred in China during 1959–1961. Under Mao Zedong's rule, tens of millions of peasants were ordered to abandon private food production and mine local deposits of iron ore and limestone, cut trees for charcoal, build clay furnaces, and smelt metal. The resulting famine led to 30 million deaths from starvation (Smil 1999).

The examples above are extreme cases. In general, nationalization programs change the structure of the economy, set into motion disruptions and shortages, and require another set of state intervention which leads to a cycle of crises. Government-induced crises are significant and consequential phenomenon. The government intervenes in the structure of the economy and disruptions occur, some manageable without deserving the label of "crisis" and others more significant. Such crises can take time to develop and to be recognized (especially by the government itself) not as a transitory accident but as a systematic problem that needs to be addressed. However, these disruptions are felt throughout the political sphere, the market, and civil society. As these disruptions occur, individuals operating in all sectors must choose how to solve the problems that arise due to the disruptions. The study of the contemporary Venezuelan crisis illustrates a contemporary example of the type of phenomenon described above in its most general features.

8.3   The Venezuelan Case

The on-going situation in Venezuela has become well known through media reports and calls for humanitarian intervention. Indeed, reports call it "a humanitarian crisis, the likes of which have never been seen in the Western Hemisphere" (PanAm Post 2016, n.p.). The Washington Post notes that, "With cash running low and debts piling up, Venezuela's socialist government has cut back sharply on food imports. And for farmers in most countries, that would present an opportunity. But this is Venezuela, whose economy operates on its own special plane of dysfunction. At a time of empty supermarkets and spreading hunger, the country's farms are producing less and less, not more, making the caloric deficit even worse" (Zuñiga and Miroff 2017, n.p.). Similarly, Aljazeera (2017, n.p.) reports that, "With much of the country on the verge of starvation, food trafficking has become one of the biggest businesses." And, "With delivery trucks under constant attack, the nation's food is now transported under armed guard. Soldiers stand watch over bakeries. The police fire rubber bullets at desperate mobs storming grocery stores, pharmacies and butcher shops," writes the *New York Times* (Casey 2016, n.p.). According to a 2016 living conditions survey conducted on 6500 Venezuelan families, three-quarters of Venezuela's population lost at least 19 pounds in body weight due to food shortages last year (Meléndez 2017). The study also found that 32.5 percent eat only once or twice a day, a three-fold increase (11.3 percent answering the same question just a year before). Further, 82 percent of Venezuelan households are estimated to live in poverty (*The Economist* 2017).

All of the above are just a sample of the ways the international media are reporting on the current developments in Venezuela. We are confronted, by all accounts, with a crisis. There are multiple ways of identifying the nature of this crisis. In fact, the most tempting is, as PanAm Post (2016) does, to call it a *humanitarian* crisis. Yet, that would be a misdiagnosis or, at least, only a partially correct diagnosis. While it is correct to say that a humanitarian crisis is taking place, what we are actually confronted with is the ultimate stage of a series of crises that are escalating to conflict and humanitarian tragedy. To correctly identify what is going on, one has to go to the roots of the problem and pinpoint the patterns of causality at work.

Upon having a closer look, what is happening in Venezuela is a typical case of a recurrent phenomenon that has been the object of many studies over the last hundred years. The phenomenon is well understood by economists: A certain set of structural changes in the economy (having to do with the property and decision rights and the freedom of exchange and association) sets into motion a series of developments that sooner or later lead to what the technical literature has called the "economy of shortage" or *shortage economy*. These structural, long-term changes are government-induced and result in dire consequences. To fully understand and respond to such crises requires recognizing the institutional reality of government-induced shortage economy, irrespective of the ideological or political labels under which the implementation of the system is presented to the public.

The notion of *shortage economy* was theorized by Janos Kornai (1980) who emphasized that a shortage economy is *a system*. Shortage economies, as Kornai demonstrated, share several characteristics out of which the central one is that the shortages are an intrinsic occurrence, and that they take place in all sectors of the economy from consumer goods and services to the means of production (Kornai 1980). A shortage is not an accidental feature or the result of a spontaneous conjuncture or contextual factors. Crises in such systems are unavoidable systemic properties. They are part and parcel of the definition and functioning of the system. A particular structure is either put in place by radical reform or gradually induced, bit by bit, until it transforms the economic system. A critical point is reached, beyond which things become acute and accelerating, pushing it past the threshold.

There is an extensive literature analyzing this type of economic system. Originating in the Austrian school of economics (Mises 1990 [1920], 1981 [1922]; Hayek 1948; Lavoie 1985; Kirzner 1988), then further developed on theoretical, empirical, and comparative lines by the field of Comparative Economic Systems, this literature has examined the structural conditions that generate such crises in various institutional and cultural environments and at different levels of development.

We understand quite well the structure and behavior of shortage economy systems. We understand—in light of the literature—the changes in property rights, decision rights, and incentives that lead to the institutionalization of the shortage economy system. If one nationalizes or otherwise centralizes the basic economic institutions of a country, and sets in place a redistributive system that undermines the productive market system, the conditions for the emergence of a shortage economy are set in place. The political or ideological label used doesn't matter. One may call it socialist, interventionist, centralized, controlled, or redistributionist. The structural features are what matter, which is the presence of systemic features that generate certain developments that lead to shortages, crises, and conflict (Ben-Ner et al. 1993; Bornstein 1989; Pryor 1970).

The frameworks developed to analyze such systems have both explanatory power and predictive capacity. These frameworks have been repeatedly tested over the years on East European socialist economies, developing world economies, and economies transitioning from socialism (see Grossman 1963, 1977; Bergson 1992; Boettke 2000, 2001). Amartya Sen (1981) has extended a version of the argument to the very problem of famines in developing societies. Given the theoretical apparatus developed by the Austrian school of economics and the field of Comparative Economics Systems as well as the existent empirical track record, the developments in Venezuela should not be surprising. There is a structural pattern we are concerned with, and we have at this stage of development in social sciences the means to identify that pattern.

In brief, for the purposes of our discussion which focuses on the responses to such crises, the key point to be distilled is that crises like the one we are witnessing in Venezuela have to be seen and treated as *structural, institutional, and economic crises*. Dealing with them as *humanitarian, conflict, and policy crises* misses the underlying systemic changes that are causing turmoil. Responses based on such misdiagnosis will not be able to address the causal roots of the phenomenon. While it is tempting to look at such crises from a humanitarian perspective—and in many cases it is unavoidable to treat them that way, especially as an immediate response, as the shortages may result in genocidal famine—the response would be inadequate if the structural cause is not addressed and removed.

Unfortunately, the theoretical and empirical understanding of the causes and nature of this type of crises continues to elude many decision makers, journalists, and the public. As noted, this specific type of crisis (or set of crises) is, however, easily predictable and preventable. And yet, again and again, one sees countries and societies engaging in costly and self-destructive experiments in implementing shortage economy system under various labels and ideological guises.

Let us now move to a second aspect of such crises by taking a closer look at the political processes in place that could help explain some characteristics of the crises as well as the responses observed in cases like the one evolving currently in Venezuela. Despite his critics, Hayek's point seems to be correct: once an economic system gets shortage economy features—either by radical reform or by gradual government intervention—and once those features become dominant, a certain political process is set into motion. The political process has to preside over a shrinking economy. Conflict over distribution becomes endemic. Once the political process reaches a threshold, escape from the shortage economy becomes increasingly difficult. Dramatic crisis and conflict become a looming presence. As long as the political actors do not address the problem at its core—that is to say the structural, systemic changes to decision and property rights—they have no choice other than to pursue conflict management and increasingly authoritarian methods. Thus, shortage economies are breeding grounds for authoritarianism. However, authoritarianism presiding over a shrinking economy is not a formula of stability. Crisis is the second nature of such a regime.

The third aspect of key interest in the context of our discussion is related to the fact that to understand such crises and the responses to them we need a dynamic rather than static framework to understand the transitions taking place, their causes, and how to respond to them. There are two kinds of transitions. The first type of transition (Type 1) proceeds as follows:

Stage 1: Market-based system.
Stage 2: Radical or gradual structural changes occur.
Stage 3: Shortage economy features appear.
Stage 4: Shortages start to develop and reach all sectors of the economy.
Stage 5: Crisis.
Stage 6: Conflict.
Stage 7: Authoritarianism.

The literature on transitions has not dedicated much attention to Type 1 transitions. However, Hayek's (1948) road to serfdom hypothesis begins to explore Type 1 transitions, and is in the end a "road to crisis" conjecture. Type 1 transitions, and Hayek's theoretical and empirical contributions on this topic, need to be better understood because in it one may identify the causal road that leads to crisis and conflict.

Instead, the literature on transitions is primarily about the reverse process: how economies get out of the shortage economy authoritarian/totalitarian trap and become developing, market economies. This is the second type of transition (Type 2). The post-communist transition offered plenty cases of reform out of the shortage economy/totalitarian equilibrium. There is a debate in that literature between two strategies of extraction from the system: gradualism vs. shock therapy or incremental vs. rapid and radical change (Boettke and Leeson 2003; Boettke 2001). That debate continues to require attention, as the issue is complex and has huge practical and moral implications. The timing and sequencing of reforms for getting out of the structural crisis trap—and all the tradeoffs involved—are issues that do not render themselves to easy solutions. The question is: What is the best way to minimize the social and human cost of getting out of the shortage economy dead end? Any approach has costs, and the costs are distributed differently and spread over time in different sequences, leading to difficult tradeoffs in reacting to such crises.

To sum up, we have a rather good understanding of the nature, structure, and dynamics of the type of crisis at work currently in Venezuela. These are structural crises of an economic and institutional nature, driven by government intervention. No amount of humanitarian aid or redistribution could solve such crises in the absence of decisive structural change. At the same time, people respond to such crises spontaneously by adjusting their behavior and strategies. Next section will focus on this sort of response and its potential for reverting the structural trend of an authoritarian shortage economy.

8.4 The Bottom-Up Response to Structural Crises Induced by Government

A shortage economy is government-induced and has long-term effects on a population. How does a bottom-up response take place in such crises? How are citizens and local communities coping with the challenges of the turmoil and shortages created by them? The people impacted by crises alter their behaviors and strategies to cope with and counter the effects (and causes) of the crisis. We again use Venezuela as a case study.

The first observation is that throughout Venezuela, people are finding solutions and ways of adjusting to the circumstances, despite the central government's attempts at command-and-control. This basic observation could be framed in organizational learning and entrepreneurship theory. Organizational learning contains both cognitive and action dimensions. It is "the acquisition of new knowledge and the translation of this knowledge into more effective organizational action" (Broekema et al. 2017, 327). An organization's structure generates how learning takes place and the decision-making apparatus determines how members of the organization respond to drastic external changes (Fiol and Lyles 1985). Such learning can be categorized as either "single-loop" or "double-loop" learning (Argyris and Schön 1978). Single-loop learning is achieved when organizational members detect problems and adjust to them without challenging or changing the basic organizational premises and norms. Under single-loop learning, minor corrections are made but an organization carries on its major objectives from the pre-crisis period. Double-loop learning inquires into and addresses broader issues of organizational objectives, norms, and working procedures. This means that old methods and objectives are discarded and new methods are adopted (Argyris and Schön 1978; Deverell 2009). This is just another—more technical—way of saying that a crisis provides the opportunity for major organizational and institutional changes. Change is a key part for institutional learning and, therefore, a crisis should be a "major initiator" for learning (Broekema et al. 2017). Overall, whether crises induce learning and in what measure that learning makes a difference is still a matter to be determined, case by case (Boin et al. 2006).

While most public administration research on crisis response and learning from crises focuses at the level of government officials, it makes sense to apply this same crisis model to the citizens who (as we will see in the case of Venezuela) are acting in spaces outside of the official governance and public administration command-and-control structure. Here, the research applying this description of entrepreneurship to crisis response becomes pivotal.

Storr, Haeffele-Balch, and Grube (2015) describe how citizens' responses can become major drivers of the general response to the crisis. The application of entrepreneurship theory by Storr, Haeffele-Balch, and

Grube helps them to illuminate the dynamics of the relevant action arenas in fresh ways. They conceptualize the entrepreneur as a combination of Kirznerian and Schumpeterian actions, seeing both views of entrepreneurship as compatible and reinforcing (Storr et al. 2015). The two ideal types are familiar. For Schumpeter (1976 [1942]), the entrepreneur innovates and creates a new "pattern of production." In doing so, the entrepreneur disrupts processes by implementing a new production method, discovering a new input to produce an existing product, and/or producing an entirely new commodity (Schumpeter 1976 [1942]). For Kirzner (1994), the entrepreneur is alert to arbitrage opportunities. He considers this alertness as the entrepreneur's primary characteristic. He is able to notice unexploited profit opportunities and, by doing so, coordinates resources that eventually make a product that consumers demand in the market (Kirzner 1994).

For Storr, Haeffele-Balch, and Grube (2015), the entrepreneur is both alert to arbitrage opportunities and this sense of alertness allows him to create new patterns. But the key step made is that they then show how their dual conceptual apparatus could be used outside of a market setting—in the public and private sector. More precisely they focus on the extreme situations of crisis to show how effective entrepreneurial actions are taking place even in such circumstances. Entrepreneurs are, thus, agents of learning. At the same time, they may be "drivers of social change." Social entrepreneurs attempt to respond to social challenges to mobilizing resources and ideas. After disasters, they can provide needed goods and services, rebuild networks between displaced survivors, and help signal that community rebuilding is underway (Storr et al. 2015).

This approach converges with insights from other lines of research on disasters and recovery. Applied social science research calls for "adaptability, creativity, and improvisation" in disaster response involving both government and private actors (Harrald 2006, 263). In general, disaster researchers have argued that the best responses to disasters involve a combination of discipline and agility. For Harrald (2006, 262), discipline is about "self-control or orderly conduct, acceptance of or submission to authority and control," and agility is being "able to move quickly and easily, deft and active." He also notes that these approaches are not mutually exclusive. He recommends a "balanced/adaptive" approach applying discipline, agility, adaptability, creativity, and improvisation as the best model (Harrald 2006, 268). This model allows social actors (both public and private) to coordinate information and resources, discern what is needed in disaster response, create an innovative solution, act in uncertain environments without having to report to a "higher up," and be agile in responding to changing circumstances. In many ways, Harrald's (2006) disaster actor reflects Storr, Haeffele-Balch, and Grube's (2015) description of what a social entrepreneur does during a crisis. Combining the attributes described by both approaches, we can not only get a better sense of how entrepreneurship operates within crises but also can understand the necessity of bringing the entrepreneurship theory apparatus to the foreground of our research.

Let us note, before moving forward, that, as Storr, Haeffele-Balch, and Grube (2015) discuss, not all entrepreneurship in disaster is "good" entrepreneurship. They write: "Of course, not all entrepreneurs should have the space to act. For instance, the entrepreneurial looter is someone whose efforts should be blocked or discouraged. Instead, it is the entrepreneurs who fulfil the roles necessary for recovery—such as providing goods and services, restoring and replacing social networks, and signaling that recovery is under way—who should be encouraged" (Storr et al. 2015, 134). A focus on entrepreneurial responses to structural crises should take this into account. Using the concept of entrepreneurship does not mean that any entrepreneurial response is by definition a constructive response to the crisis.

Using the theoretical lenses brought by entrepreneurship theory gives an additional dimension and significance to the multitude of ways people cope with the shortages and problems created by structural crises. In terms of public policy and public administration, however, evidence shows that learning (at least at the level of government actors) may not follow from a crisis (Keeler 1993; Sabatier and Jenkins-Smith 1993; Kingdon 1995; Birkland 2006). Or that incentives for status quo maintenance are so powerful that they offset the decision makers learning processes. Yet citizens simply cannot afford to embrace status quo and circumvent learning.

In the case of Venezuela, government actors use force to quell dissidents during the crisis (Casey and Herrero 2017) instead of actively engaging "double-loop" learning with a view to changing the structure of the situation generating the problem. However, at the same time, learning and adaptation is occurring among private citizens actively solving problems during the crisis. While the Maduro government is aggravating the crisis through the use of force, social actors are trying to learn how to adjust to the new circumstances and acting, as described by Harrald (2006, 262), as "quickly and easily, deft and active" to respond to specific challenges created by the crisis. Additionally, these bottom-up responses may also provide an opportunity for double-loop learning, where individuals actively question the underlying norms and practices that generate the crisis. That is precisely the type of learning which can create an avenue for a Type 2 transition—creating the precondition for addressing the real causes of the crisis.

To illustrate these points, let us start with the observation that a shortage economy generates a food shortage. In the Venezuela case, prior to the economic collapse, many Venezuelans found that smuggling goods into neighboring Colombia could earn them more money than working a "regular job" (Ulmer and Polanco 2016). But now that there is a massive shortage of food, Venezuelans use the same networks to buy these basic necessities from people in Colombia (Ulmer and Polanco 2016). Individuals from both countries are coordinating in spontaneous ways to combat the food shortages in Venezuela. It is important to note that people are using already established smuggling routes to exploit arbitrage opportunities that help themselves and their communities. At the same time, sellers in Colombia are recognizing the arbitrage opportunities to sell to Venezuelan customers with high demand for food. Now that shortages are rampant in Venezuela, entrepreneurs made an adjustment and redirected the flow of goods along the same smuggling channels (single-loop learning).

In response to smuggling, the Maduro government has cracked down on border enforcement. However, smugglers use political corruption (i.e. bribes) to their advantage to guarantee safe passage across the border and bring in much demanded food. One smuggler in Paraguachon (a town along Venezuela's western border) told reporters, "We pay the National Guard a few thousand bolivars to get across, depending on what we have in the truck" (Gupta 2016, n.p.). These border guards are alert to the smuggling and see this as an opportunity to earn additional income. In this "single-loop" learning situation, relationships between smugglers and board guards are changed to allow for goods to flow into Venezuela to meet demand.

This is an example of entrepreneurship which is a bottom-up, positive contribution, mitigating the effects of the shortage economy imposed in the country by the political leaders. It provides much needed goods to a population deprived of food and other resources. At the same time, it is further undermining the structure and legitimacy of the government by increasing the disconnect between what government says (the rhetoric of "anti-corruption") reinforced by initiatives of increasing border security to stop smugglers, and the reality on the ground (bribes to border control to allow smuggling to still occur). In a situation where the government is attempting to tighten its control over economic life, these private and public actors are coordinating in ways that solve the food shortages and further undermine the very legitimacy of the regime.

Black markets in medicine are another example. Medicine, like food, often becomes extremely scarce in a shortage economy. This has given rise to "medical flea markets" where venders sell everything from vitamins to antibiotics to contraceptives in an open-air marketplace. These medications are usually smuggled in from Colombia through the same networks described above used to smuggle food (Polanco and Urrutia 2017). Drugs are often sold next to vegetables but are often not properly packaged or stored. When faced with a choice of consuming medicine that may not be properly stored or not getting any medical treatment, many choose to assume the risk. Norkis Pabon, a citizen interviewed by Reuters, looked for medication for her hospitalized husband to prevent his foot injury from getting worse from diabetes (Polanco and Urrutia 2017). Pabon chose to purchase black market medication to help treat her husband rather than risk no treatment at all. Again, entrepreneurs are finding arbitrage opportunities to sell goods in an open market, including food and medicine.

So far, we have explored a range of ways people respond to their circumstances during a Type 1 transition. Fortunately, Type 2 transitions may emerge from the very reactions and strategies people develop to respond to crisis. Shortage economies (in most cases governed through authoritarian political rule) may be able to transition to market economies, by building upon the practices and learning induced by the crisis. In this respect one could see how the government-induced crisis prompts a double-loop learning process. People may begin to question the norms and underlying methods of the governance systems (in Venezuela, the socialist government). While the system once provided citizens with lower-cost food and necessities, these policies led to shortages and resulted in further government intervention and control. More government intervention of the same kind, however, is not a viable solution. Thus, as a crisis gets worse, it may be able to prompt a change in how people view (based on their experiences) their government and the governance systems currently in place and may lead to structural changes.

While Venezuelans are not likely spending their time reading economic theory or history, they are actively engaging in market and social exchanges and finding ways to cope with and counter the effects of the crisis. This allows them to both survive the crisis and start thinking about alternatives (Enia 2018), and a Type 2 transition becomes much more feasible. And thus, the bottom-up response to structural government-induced crises may not only help to identify solutions to specific problems of daily life during crises, but also create the conditions for large-scale, structural solutions.

8.5   Conclusion

We understand relatively well the processes leading to structural, government-induced economic crises and we have a good understanding of viable solutions for long-term change. Bottom-up responses may take many forms and are a natural, spontaneous way of dealing with crises, often using networks and skills established prior to the economic crisis to meet the needs of everyday life. These responses may also generate longer-term change. But irrespective of the speed of recovery (be it from the top down or bottom up), once a government-induced crisis begins, there are unavoidable social and human costs.

Further, we have intellectual tools and the knowledge to predict the patterns and prevent such crises from occurring, yet such crises happen again and again (such as in the current case of Venezuela). The lesson is this: It is not sufficient to merely understand the causes and nature of such crises as well as the optimal strategies of response to such crises. Something else, an additional element—a missing argument or missing factor—has to be brought into the picture in order to prevent such unfortunate phenomena and situations. That element—a commitment to upholding the institutions that bring about growth and stability and dismissing the institutions that lead to government-induced crises—needs to spread through to the ethos of the elites, the prevailing public philosophy, the public opinion of individual citizens and their communities, and the institutional arrangements. Irrespective of its nature, its public support is an important act of social and political entrepreneurship of great civic importance.

References

Aljazeera. 2017. Venezuela Military Controls Food as Nation Goes Hungry. *Aljazeera*, January 1. https://www.aljazeera.com/news/2017/01/venezuela-military-controls-food-nation-hungry-170101195414433.html.

Argyris, C., and D. Schön. 1978. *Organizational Learning*. Reading, MA: Addison & Wesley.

Baumgartner, F.R., and B.D. Jones. 1993. *Agendas and Instability in American Politics*. Chicago: University of Chicago Press.

Ben-Ner, A., J.M. Montias, and E. Neuberger. 1993. Basic Issues in Organizations: A Comparative Perspective. *Journal of Comparative Economics* 17 (2): 207–242.

Bergson, A. 1992. Communist Economic Efficiency Revisited. *The American Economic Review* 82 (2): 27–30.

Birkland, T.A. 2006. *Lessons of Disaster: Policy Change after Catastrophic Events*. Washington, DC: Georgetown University Press.

Boettke, P.J. 2000. *Socialism and the Market: The Socialist Calculation Debate Revisited*. 9 vols. New York: Routledge.

———. 2001. *Calculation and Coordination: Essays on Socialism and Transitional Political Economy*. New York: Routledge.

Boettke, P.J., and P.T. Leeson. 2003. Is the Transition to the Market too Important to Be Left to the Market? *Economic Affairs* 23 (1): 33–39.

Boin, A., P. Hart, E. Stern, and B. Sundelius. 2006. *The Politics of Crisis Management: Public Leadership under Pressure.* New York: Cambridge University Press.

Bornstein, M., ed. 1989. *Comparative Economic Systems: Models and Cases.* 7th ed. Burr Ridge, IL: Irwin Professional Publishing.

Broekema, W., D. van Kleef, and T. Steen. 2017. Organizational Learning from Crisis? Insights from the Dutch Food Safety Services' Response to Four Veterinary Crises. *Journal of Contingencies and Crisis Management* 25 (4): 326–340.

Casey, N. 2016. Venezuelans Ransack Stores as Hunger Grips the Nation. *The New York Times*, June 19. https://www.nytimes.com/2016/06/20/world/americas/venezuelans-ransack-stores-as-hunger-stalks-crumbling-nation.html.

Casey, N., and A.V. Herrero. 2017. Venezuela's New Assembly Members Share a Goal: Stifle Dissent. *The New York Times*, August 3. https://www.nytimes.com/2017/08/03/world/americas/venezuela-constituent-assembly-members-maduro.html.

Deverell, E. 2009. Crises as Learning Triggers: Exploring a Conceptual Framework of Crisis-induced Learning. *Journal of Contingencies and Crisis Management* 17 (3): 185–186.

Enia, J. 2018. Do Contracts Save Lives? The Relationship Between Contract Intensive Economies and Natural Disaster Fatalities. *Risk, Hazards & Crisis in Public Policy* 9 (1): 60–81.

Fiol, C.M., and M.A. Lyles. 1985. Organizational Learning. *Academy of Management Review* 10 (4): 803–813.

Grossman, G. 1963. Notes for a Theory of the Command Economy. *Soviet Studies* 15 (2): 101–123.

———. 1977. The Second Economy of the USSR. *Problems of Communism* 26 (5): 25–40.

Gupta, G. 2016. Smuggling Soars as Venezuela's Economy Sink. *Reuters*, January 20. https://www.reuters.com/article/us-venezuela-smuggling-insight/smuggling-soars-as-venezuelas-economy-sinks-idUSKCN0UY1IT.

Harrald, J. 2006. Agility and Discipline: Critical Success Factors for Disaster Response. *Annals of the American Academy of Political Science* 604 (1): 256–272.

Hayek, F.A. 1948. *Individualism and Economic Order.* Chicago: University of Chicago Press.

Higgs, R. 1987. *Crisis and Leviathan: Critical Episodes in the Growth of American Government*. New York: Oxford University Press.

Keeler, J.T.S. 1993. Opening the Window for Reform: Mandates, Crises, and Extraordinary Policy-Making. *Comparative Political Studies* 25 (4): 433–486.

Kingdon, J. 1995. *Agendas, Alternatives, and Public Policies*. 2nd ed. Boston: Little, Brown.

Kirzner, I.M. 1988. The Economic Calculation Debate: Lessons for Austrians. *Review of Austrian Economics* 2 (1): 1–18.

———. 1994. Entrepreneurship. In *The Edgar Companion to Austrian Economics*, ed. P.J. Boettke, 103–111. Northampton: Edward Elgar Publishing Inc.

Kornai, J. 1980. *Economics of Shortage*. Amsterdam: North Holland Press.

Lavoie, D. 1985. *Rivalry and Central Planning: The Socialist Calculation Debate Revisited*. New York: Cambridge University Press.

Meléndez, L. 2017. Encovi 2016: 74% of Venezuelans Lost More than 8 Kilos in Weight Last Year. *Runrun.es*, February 18. https://runrun.es/investigacion/297797/encovi-2016-74-de-los-venezolanos-perdio-mas-de-8-kilos-de-peso-el-ano-pasado/.

Mises, L. 1981 [1922]. *Socialism: An Economic and Sociological Critique*. Indianapolis, IN: Liberty Fund, Inc.

———. 1990 [1920]. *Economic Calculation in the Socialist Commonwealth*. Auburn, AL: Mises Institute.

Olson, M. 1982. *The Rise and Decline of Nations: Economic Growth, Stagflation, and Social Rigidities*. New Haven: Yale University Press.

PanAm Post. 2016. Venezuela: Mass Famine Is Imminent as Neighbors, Washington Stand By. *PanAm Post*, June 22. https://panampost.com/panam-staff/2016/06/22/venezuela-mass-famine-is-imminent-as-neighbors-washington-stand-by/?cn-reloaded=1.

Pauchant, T.C., and I.I. Mitroff. 1992. *Transforming the Crisis Prone Organization*. San Francisco: Jossey-Bass Publishers.

Polanco, A., and I. Urrutia. 2017. Venezuela's Chronic Shortages Give Rise to 'Medical Flea Markets'. *Reuters*, December 8. https://www.reuters.com/article/us-venezuela-medicine/venezuelas-chronic-shortages-give-rise-to-medical-flea-markets-idUSKBN1E21J4.

Pryor, F.L. 1970. Barriers to Market Socialism in Eastern Europe in the Mid-1960. *Studies in Comparative Communism* 3 (2): 31–64.

Rosenthal, U., A.R. Boin, and L.K. Comfort. 2001. *Managing Crises: Threats, Dilemmas, Opportunities*. Springfield: Charles C Thomas Publishing Ltd.

Sabatier, P.A., and H.C. Jenkins-Smith. 1993. *Policy Change and Learning: An Advocacy Coalition Approach.* Boulder, CO: Westview Press.

Schumpeter, J. 1976 [1942]. *Capitalism, Socialism and Democracy.* London: George Allen & Unwin.

Sen, A. 1981. Ingredients of Famine Analysis: Availability and Entitlements. *The Quarterly Journal of Economics* 96 (3): 433–464.

Smil, V. 1999. China's Great Famine: 40 Years Later. *BMJ* 319 (18–25): 1619–1621.

Storr, V.H., S. Haeffele-Balch, and L.E. Grube. 2015. *Community Revival in the Wake of Disaster: Lessons in Local Entrepreneurship.* New York: Palgrave Macmillan.

The Economist. 2017. Will Venezuela's Dictatorship Survey? *The Economist,* March 9. https://www.economist.com/the-americas/2017/03/09/will-venezuelas-dictatorship-survive.

Ulmer, A., and A. Polanco. 2016. In Switch, Hungry Venezuelans Now Smuggle Colombian Food Home. *Reuters,* June 8. https://www.reuters.com/article/us-venezuela-smuggling-widerimage/in-switch-hungry-venezuelans-now-smuggle-colombian-food-home-idUSKCN0YU1WA.

US Commission on the Ukrainian Famine. 1988. *Investigations of the Ukrainian Famine, 1932–1933: Report to Congress.* Washington, DC: US Congress.

Zuñiga, M., and N. Miroff. 2017. Venezuela's Paradox: People Are Hungry, But Farmers Can't Feed Them. *The Washington Post,* May 22. https://www.washingtonpost.com/world/the_americas/venezuelas-paradox-people-are-hungry-but-farmers-cant-feed-them/2017/05/21/ce460726-3987-11e7-a59b-26e0451a96fd_story.html?noredirect=on&utm_term=.b176b12dbd6b.

Index[1]

---

[1] Note: Page numbers followed by 'n' refer to notes.

9 783030 393113